Database Design Using Entity-Relationship Diagrams

Database Design Using Entity-Relationship Diagrams

Sikha Bagui and **Richard Earp**

AUERBACH PUBLICATIONS

A CRC Press Company
Boca Raton   London   New York   Washington, D.C.

Library of Congress Cataloging-in-Publication Data

Bagui, Sikha, 1964-
  Database design using entity-relationship diagrams / Sikha Bagui, Richard Earp.
      p.   cm. -- (Foundation of database design ; 1)
  Includes bibliographical references and index.
  ISBN 0-8493-1548-4 (alk. paper)
    1. Database design. 2. Relational databases. I. Earp, Richard, 1940- II. Title. III. Series.

QA76.9.D26B35 2003
  005.74--dc21
                                                                    2003041804

Visit the Auerbach Web site at www.auerbach-publications.com

© 2003 by CRC Press LLC
Auerbach is an imprint of CRC Press LLC

No claim to original U.S. Government works
International Standard Book Number 0-8493-1548-4
Library of Congress Card Number 2003041804
Printed in the United States of America 1 2 3 4 5 6 7 8 9 0
Printed on acid-free paper

Dedication

Dedicated to my father, Santosh Saha, and mother, Ranu Saha
and
my husband, Subhash Bagui
and
my sons, Sumon and Sudip
and
Pradeep and Priyashi Saha

S.B.

To my wife, Brenda,
and
my children: Beryl, Rich, Gen, and Mary Jo

R.E.

Contents

Preface

Data modeling and database design have undergone significant evolution in recent years. Today, the relational data model and the relational database system dominate business applications. The relational model has allowed the database designer to focus on the logical and physical characteristics of a database separately. This book concentrates on techniques for database design, with a very strong bias for relational database systems, using the ER (Entity Relationships) approach for conceptual modeling (solely a logical implementation).

Intended Audience

This book is intended to be used by database practitioners and students for data modeling. It is also intended to be used as a supplemental text in database courses, systems analysis and design courses, and other courses that design and implement databases. Many present-day database and systems analysis and design books limit their coverage of data modeling. This book not only increases the exposure to data modeling concepts, but also presents a detailed, step-by-step approach to designing an ER diagram and developing the relational database from it.

Book Highlights

This book focuses on presenting: (1) an ***ER design methodology*** for developing an ER diagram; (2) a ***grammar*** for the ER diagrams that can be presented back to the user; and (3) ***mapping rules*** to map the ER diagram to a relational database. The steps for the ER design methodology, the grammar for the ER diagrams, as well as the mapping rules are developed and presented in a systematic, step-by-step manner throughout the book. Also, several examples of "sample data" have been included with relational database mappings — all to give a "realistic" feeling.

This book is divided into ten chapters. The first chapter gives the reader some background by introducing some relational database concepts such as functional dependencies and database normalization. The ER design methodology and mapping rules are presented, starting in Chapter 2.

Chapter 2 introduces the concepts of the entity, attributes, relationships, and the "one-entity" ER diagram. Steps 1, 2, and 3 of the ER Design Methodology are developed. The "one-entity" grammar and mapping rules for the "one-entity" diagram are presented.

Chapter 3 extends the one-entity diagram to include a second entity. The concept of testing attributes for entities is discussed and relationships between the entities are developed. Steps 3a, 3b, 4, 5, and 6 of the ER design methodology are developed, and grammar for the ER diagrams developed up to this point is presented.

Chapter 4 discusses structural constraints in relationships. Several examples are given of 1:1, 1:M, and M:N relationships. Step 6 of the ER design methodology is revised and step 7 is developed. A grammar for the structural constraints and the mapping rules is also presented.

Chapter 5 develops the concept of the weak entity. This chapter revisits and revises steps 3 and 4 of the ER design methodology to include the weak entity. Again, a grammar and the mapping rules for the weak entity are presented.

Chapter 6 discusses and extends different aspects of binary relationships in ER diagrams. This chapter revises step 5 to include the concept of more than one relationship, and revises step 6(b) to include derived and redundant relationships. The concept of the recursive relationship is introduced in this chapter. The grammar and mapping rules for recursive relationships are presented.

Chapter 7 discusses ternary and other "higher-order" relationships. Step 6 of the ER design methodology is again revised to include ternary and other, higher-order relationships. Several examples are given, and the grammar and mapping rules are developed and presented.

Chapter 8 discusses generalizations and specializations. Once again, step 6 of the ER design methodology is modified to include generalizations and specializations, and the grammar and mapping rules for generalizations and specializations are presented.

Chapter 9 provides a summary of the mapping rules and reverse-engineering from a relational database to an ER diagram.

Chapters 2 through 9 present ER diagrams using a Chen-like model. Chapter 10 discusses the Barker/Oracle-like models, highlighting the main similarities and differences between the Chen-like model and the Barker/Oracle-like model.

Every chapter presents several examples. "Checkpoint" sections within the chapters and end-of-chapter exercises are presented in every chapter to be worked out by the students — to get a better understanding of the material within the respective sections and chapters. At the end of most chapters, there is a running case study with the solution (i.e., the ER diagram and the relational database with some sample data).

Acknowledgments

Our special thanks are due to Rich O'Hanley, President, Auerbach Publications, for his continuous support during this project. We would also like to thank Gerry Jaffe, Project Editor; Shayna Murry, Cover Designer; Will Palmer, Prepress Technician, and James Yanchak, Electronic Production Manager, for their help with the production of this book.

Finally, we would like to thank Dr. Ed Rodgers, Chairman, Department of Computer Science, University of West Florida, for his continuing support, and Dr. Jim Bezdek, for encouraging us to complete this book.

Introduction

This book was written to aid students in database classes and to help database practitioners in understanding how to arrive at a definite, clear database design using an entity relationship (ER) diagram. In designing a database with an ER diagram, we recognize that this is but one way to arrive at the objective — the database. There are other design methodologies that also produce databases, but an ER diagram is the most common. The ER diagram (also called an ERD) is a subset of what are called "semantic models." As we proceed through this material, we will occasionally point out where other models differ from the ER model.

The ER model is one of the best-known tools for logical database design. Within the database community it is considered to be a very natural and easy-to-understand way of conceptualizing the structure of a database. Claims that have been made for it include: (1) it is simple and easily understood by non-specialists; (2) it is easily conceptualized, the basic constructs (entities and relationships) are highly intuitive and thus provide a very natural way of representing a user's information requirements; and (3) it is a model that describes a world in terms of entities and attributes that is most suitable for computer-naïve end users. In contrast, many educators have reported that students in database courses have difficulty grasping the concepts of the ER approach and, in particular, applying them to the real-world problems (Goldstein and Storey, 1990).

We took the approach of starting with an entity, and then developing from it in an "inside-out strategy" (as mentioned in Elmasri and Navathe, 2000). Software engineering involves eliciting from (perhaps) "naïve" users what they would like to have stored in an information system. The process we presented follows the software engineering paradigm of requirements/specifications, with the ER diagram being the core of the specification. Designing a software solution depends on correct elicitation. In most software engineering paradigms, the process starts with a requirements elicitation, followed by a specification and then a feedback loop. In plain English, the idea is (1) "tell me what you want" (requirements), and then (2) "this is what I think you want" (specification). This process of requirements/specification can (and probably should) be iterative so that users understand what they will get from the system and analysts will understand what the users want.

A methodology for producing an ER diagram is presented. The process leads to an ER diagram that is then translated into plain (but meant to be precise) English that a user can understand. The iterative mechanism then takes over to arrive at a specification (a revised ER diagram and English) that both users and analysts understand. The mapping of the ER diagram into a relational database is presented; mapping to other logical database models is not covered. We feel that the relational database is most appropriate to demonstrate mapping because it is the most-used contemporary database model. Actually, the idea behind the ER diagram is to produce a high-level database model that has no particular logical model implied (relational, hierarchical, object oriented, or network).

We have a strong bias toward the *relational model*. The "goodness" of the final relational model is testable via the ideas of normal forms. The goodness of the relational model produced by a mapping from an ER diagram theoretically should be guaranteed by the mapping process. If a diagram is "good enough," then the mapping to a "good" relational model should happen almost automatically. In practice, the scenario will be to produce as good an ER diagram as possible, map it to a relational model, and then shift the discussion to "is this a good relational model or not?" using the theory of normal forms and other associated criteria of "relational goodness."

The approach to database design taken will be intuitive and informal. We do not deal with precise definitions of set relations. We use the intuitive "one/many" for cardinality and "may/must" for participation constraints. The intent is to provide a mechanism to produce an ER diagram that can be presented to a user in English, and to polish the diagram into a specification that can then be mapped into a database. We then suggest testing the produced database by the theory of normal forms and other criteria (i.e., referential integrity constraints). We also suggest a reverse-mapping paradigm for mapping a relational database back to an ER diagram for the purpose of documentation.

The ER Models We Chose

We begin this venture into ER diagrams with a "Chen-like" model, and most of this book (Chapters 2 through 9) is written using the Chen-like model. Why did we choose this model? Chen (1976) introduced the idea of ER diagrams (Elmasri and Navathe, 2000), and most database texts use some variant of the Chen model. Chen and others have improved the ER process over the years; and while there is no standard ER diagram (ERD) model, the Chen-like model and variants thereof are common, particularly in comprehensive database texts. Chapter 10 briefly introduces the "Barker/Oracle-like" model. As with the Chen model, we do not follow the Barker or Oracle models precisely, and hence we will use the term Barker/Oracle-like models in this text.

There are also other reasons for choosing the Chen-like model over the other models. With the Chen-like model, one need not consider how the database will be implemented. The Barker-like model is more intimately tied to the relational database paradigm. Oracle Corporation uses an ERD that is closer to the Barker model. Also, in the Barker-like and Oracle-like ERD, there is no accommodation for some of the features we present in the Chen-like model. For example, multi-valued attributes and weak entities are not part of the Barker- or Oracle-like design process.

The process of database design follows the software engineering paradigm; and during the requirements and specifications phase, sketches of ER diagrams will be made and remade. It is not at all unusual to arrive at a design and then revise it. In developing ER models, one needs to realize that the Chen model is developed to be independent of implementation. The Chen-like model is used almost exclusively by universities in database instruction. The mapping rules of the Chen model to a relational database are relatively straightforward, but the model itself does not represent any particular logical model. Although the Barker/Oracle-like model is quite popular, it is implementation dependent upon knowledge of relational databases. The Barker/Oracle model maps directly to a relational database; there are no real mapping rules for that model.

References

Elmasri, R. and Navathe, S.B., *Fundamentals of Database Systems*, 3rd ed., Addison-Wesley, Reading, MA, 2000.

Goldstein, R.C. and Storey, V.C., "Some Findings on the Intuitiveness of Entity Relationship Constructs," in Lochovsky, F.H., Ed., *Entity-Relationship Approach to Database Design and Querying*, Elsevier Science, New York, 1990.

Chapter 1

The Software Engineering Process and Relational Databases

Chapter Topics

This chapter introduces some concepts that are essential to our presentation of the design of the database. We begin by introducing the idea of "software engineering" — a process of specifying systems and writing software. We then take up the subject of relational databases. Most databases in use today are relational, and the focus in this book will be to design a relational database. Before we can actually get into relational databases, we introduce the idea of functional dependencies (FDs). Once we have accepted the notion of functional dependencies, we can then easily define what is a good (and a not-so-good) database.

What Is the Software Engineering Process?

The term "software engineering" refers to a process of specifying, designing, writing, delivering, maintaining, and finally retiring software. There are many excellent references on the topic of software engineering (Schach, 1999). Some authors use the term "software engineering" synonymously with "systems analysis and design" and other titles, but the underlying point is that any information system requires some process to develop it correctly. Software engineering spans a wide range of information system problems. The problem of primary interest here is that of specifying a database. "Specifying a database" means that we will document what the database is supposed to contain.

A basic idea in software engineering is that to build software correctly, a series of steps (or phases) are required. The steps ensure that a process of thinking precedes action — thinking through "what is needed" precedes "what is written." Further, the "thinking before action" necessitates that all parties involved in software development understand and communicate with one another. One common version of presenting the thinking before acting scenario is referred to as a *waterfall model* (Schach, 1999), as the process is supposed to flow in a directional way without retracing.

An early step in the software engineering process involves specifying what is to be done. The waterfall model implies that once the specification of the software is written, it is not changed, but rather used as a basis for development. One can liken the software engineering exercise to building a house. The specification is the "what do you want in your house" phase. Once agreed upon, the next step is design. As the house is designed and the blueprint is drawn, it is not acceptable to revisit the specification except for minor alterations. There has to be a meeting of the minds at the end of the specification phase to move along with the design (the blueprint) of the house to be constructed. So it is with software and database development.

Software production is a life-cycle process — it is created, used, and eventually retired. The "players" in the software development life cycle can be placed into two camps, often referred to as the "user" and the "analyst." Software is designed by the analyst for the user according to the user's specification. In our presentation we will think of ourselves as the analyst trying to enunciate what the users think they want.

There is no general agreement among software engineers as to the exact number of steps or phases in the waterfall-type software development "model." Models vary, depending on the interest of the author in one part or another in the process. A very brief description of the software process goes like this:

Step 1 (or Phase 1): Requirements. Find out what the user wants or needs.

Step 2: Specification. Write out the user wants or needs as precisely as possible.

> *Step 2a: Feedback the specification to the user* (a review) to see if the analyst (you) have it right.
>
> *Step 2b: Re-do the specification as necessary and return to step 2a* until analyst and user both understand one another and agree to move on.

Step 3: Software is designed to meet the specification from step 2.

> *Step 3a: Software design is independently checked against the specification* and fixed until the analyst has clearly met the specification. Note the sense of agreement in step 2 and the use of step 2 as a basis for further action. When step 3 begins, going back up the waterfall is difficult — it is supposed to be that way. Perhaps minor specification details might be revisited but the idea is to move on once each step is finished.

Step 4: Software is written (developed).

> *Step 4a: Software, as written, is checked against the design* until the analyst has clearly met the design. Note that the specification in step 2 is long past and only minor modifications of the design would be tolerated here.

Step 5: Software is turned over to the user to be used in the application.

> *Step 5a: User tests and accepts or rejects until software is written correctly* (it meets specification and design).

Step 6: Maintenance is performed on software until it is retired. Maintenance is a very time-consuming and expensive part of the software process — particularly if the software engineering process has not been done well. Maintenance involves correcting hidden software faults as well as enhancing the functionality of the software.

ER Diagrams and the Software Engineering Life Cycle

This text concentrates on steps 1 through 3 of the software life cycle for database modeling. A database is a collection of related data. The concept of related data means that a database stores information about one enterprise — a business, an organization, a grouping of related people or processes. For example, a database might be about Acme Plumbing and involve customers and production. A different database might be one about the members and activities of the "Over 55 Club" in town. It would be inappropriate to have data about the "Over 55 Club" and Acme Plumbing in the same database because the two organizations are not related. Again, a database is a collection of *related* data.

Database systems are often modeled using an Entity Relationship (ER) diagram as the "blueprint" from which the actual data is stored — the output of the design phase. The ER diagram is an analyst's tool to diagram the data to –be stored in an information system. Step 1, the requirements phase, can be quite frustrating as the analyst must elicit needs and wants from the user. The user may or may not be computer-sophisticated and may or may not know a software system's capabilities. The analyst often has a difficult time deciphering needs and wants to strike a balance of specifying something realistic.

In the real world, the "user" and the "analyst" can be committees of professionals but the idea is that users (or user groups) must convey their ideas to an analyst (or team of analysts) — users must express what they want and think they need.

User descriptions are often vague and unstructured. We will present a methodology that is designed to make the analyst's language precise enough so that the user is comfortable with the to-be-designed database, and the analyst has a tool that can be mapped directly into a database.

The early steps in the software engineering life cycle for databases would be to:

> *Step 1: Getting the requirements.* Here, we listen and ask questions about what the user wants to store. This step often involves letting users describe how they intend to use the data that you (the analyst) will load into a database. There is often a learning curve necessary for the analyst as the user explains the system they know so well to a person who is ignorant of their specific business.
>
> *Step 2: Specifying the database.* This step involves grammatical descriptions and diagrams of what the analyst thinks the user wants. Because most users are unfamiliar with the notion of an Entity-Relationship diagram (ERD), our methodology will supplement the ERD with grammatical descriptions of what the database is supposed to contain and how the parts of the database relate to one another. The technical description of the database is often dry and uninteresting to a user; however, when analysts put what they think they heard into statements, the user and the analyst have a "meeting of the minds." For example, if the analyst makes statements such as, "All employees must generate invoices," the user may then affirm, deny, or modify the declaration to fit what is actually the case.
>
> *Step 3: Designing the database.* Once the database has been diagrammed and agreed-to, the ERD becomes the blueprint for constructing the database.

Checkpoint 1.1

1. Briefly describe the steps of the software engineering life-cycle process.
2. Who are the two main players in the software development life cycle?

Data Models

Data must be stored in some fashion in a file for it to be useful. In database circles over the past 20 years or so, there have been three basic camps of "logical" database models — hierarchical, network, and relational — three ways of logically perceiving the arrangement of data in the file structure. This section provides some insight into each of these three main models along with a brief introduction to the relational model.

The Hierarchical Model

The idea in hierarchical models is that all data is arranged in a hierarchical fashion (a.k.a. a parent–child relationship). If, for example, we had a database for a company and there was an employee who had dependents, then one would think of an employee as the "parent" of the dependent. (Note: Understand that the parent–child relationship is not meant to be a human relationship. The term "parent–child" is simply a convenient reference to a common familial relationship. The "child" here could be a dependent spouse or any other human relationship.) We could have every dependent with one employee parent and every employee might have multiple dependent children. In a database, information is organized into files, records, and fields. Imagine a file cabinet we call the employee file: it contains all information about employees of the company. Each employee has an employee record, so the employee file consists of individual employee records. Each record in the file would be expected to be organized in a similar way. For example, you would expect that the person's name would be in the same place in each record. Similarly, you would expect that the address, phone number, etc. would be found in the same place in everyone's records. We call the name a "field" in a record. Similarly, the address, phone number, salary, date of hire, etc. are also fields in the employee's record. You can imagine that a parent (employee) record might contain all sorts of fields — different companies have different needs and no two companies are exactly alike.

In addition to the employee record, we will suppose in this example that the company also has a dependent file with dependent information in it — perhaps the dependent's name, date of birth, place of birth, school attending, insurance information, etc. Now imagine that you have two file cabinets: one for employees and one for dependents. The connection between the records in the different file cabinets is called a "relationship." Each dependent must be related to some employee, and each employee may or may not have a dependent in the dependent file cabinet.

Relationships in all database models have what are called "structural constraints." A structural constraint consists of two notions: cardinality and optionality. Cardinality is a description of how many of one record type relate to the other, and vice versa. In our company, if an employee can have multiple dependents and the dependent can have only one employee parent, we would say the relationship is one-to-many — that is, one employee, many dependents. If the company is such that employees might have multiple dependents and a dependent might be claimed by more that one employee, then the cardinality would be many-to-many — many employees, many dependents. Optionality refers to whether or not one record may or must have a corresponding record in the other file. If the employee may or may not have dependents, then the optionality of the employee to dependent relationship is "optional" or "partial." If the dependents must be "related to" employee(s), then the optionality of dependent to employee is "mandatory" or "full."

Furthermore, relationships are always stated in both directions in a database description. We could say that:

Employees may have zero or more dependents

and

Dependents must be associated with one and only one employee.

Note the employee-to-dependent, one-to-many cardinality and the optional/ mandatory nature of the relationship.

All relationships between records in a hierarchical model have a cardinality of one-to-many or one-to-one, but never many-to-one or many-to-many. So, for a hierarchical model of employee and dependent, we can only have the employee-to-dependent relationship as one-to-many or one-to-one; an employee may have zero or more dependents, or (unusual as it might be) an employee may have one and only one dependent. In the hierarchical model, you could not have dependents with multiple parent–employees.

The original way hierarchical databases were implemented involved choosing some way of physically "connecting" the parent and the child records. Imagine you have looked up an employee in the employee filing cabinet and you want to find the dependent records for that employee in the dependent filing cabinet. One way to implement the employee–dependent relationship would be to have an employee record point to a dependent record and have that dependent record point to the next dependent (a linked list of child –records, if you will). For example, you find employee Jones. In Jones' record, there is a notation that Jones' first dependent is found in the dependent filing cabinet, file drawer 2, record 17. The "file drawer 2, record 17" is called a pointer and is the "connection" or "relationship" between the employee and the dependent. Now to take this example further, suppose the record of the dependent in file drawer 2, record 17 points to the next dependent in file drawer 3, record 38; then that person points to the next dependent in file drawer 1, record 82.

In the linked list approach to connecting parent and child records, there are advantages and disadvantages to that system. For example, one advantage would be that each employee has to maintain only one pointer and that the size of the "linked list" of dependents is theoretically unbounded. Drawbacks would include the fragility of the system in that if one dependent record is destroyed, then the chain is broken. Further, if you wanted information about only one of the child records, you might have to look through many records before you find the one you are looking for.

There are, of course, several other ways of making the parent–child link. Each method has advantages and disadvantages, but imagine the difficulty with the linked list system if you wanted to have multiple parents for each child record. Also note that some system must be chosen to be implemented in the underlying database software. Once the linking system is chosen, it is fixed by the software implementation; the way the link is done has to be used to link all child records to parents, regardless of how inefficient it might be for one situation.

There are three major drawbacks to the hierarchical model:

1. Not all situations fall into the one-to-many, parent–child format.
2. The choice of the way in which the files are linked impacts performance, both positively and negatively.
3. The linking of parent and child records is done physically. If the dependent file were reorganized, then all pointers would have to be reset.

The Network Model

The network model was developed as a successor to the hierarchical model. The network model alleviated the first concern as in the network model — one was not restricted to having one parent per child — a many-to-many relationship or a many-to-one relationship was acceptable. For example, suppose that our database consisted of our employee–dependent situation as in the hierarchical model, plus we had another relationship that involved a "school attended" by the dependent. In this case, the employee–dependent relationship might still be one-to-many, but the "school attended"–dependent relationship might well be many-to-many. A dependent could have two "parent/schools." To implement the dependent–school relationship in hierarchical databases involved creating redundant files, because for each school, you would have to list all dependents. Then, each dependent who attended more than one school would be listed twice or three times, once for each school. In network databases we could simply have two connections or links from the dependent child to each school, and vice versa.

The second and third drawbacks of hierarchical databases spilled over to network databases. If one were to write a database system, one would have to choose some method of physically connecting or linking records. This choice of record connection then locks us into the same problem as before, a hardware-implemented connection that impacts performance both positively and negatively. Further, as the database becomes more complicated, the paths of connections and the maintenance problems become exponentially more difficult to manage.

The Relational Model

E. Codd (ca. 1970) introduced the relational model to describe a database that did not suffer from the drawbacks of the hierarchical and network models. Codd's premise was that if we ignore the way data files are connected and arrange our data into simple two-dimensional, unordered tables, then we can develop a calculus for queries (questions posed to the database) and focus on the data as data, not as a physical realization of a logical model. Codd's idea was truly logical in that one was no longer concerned with how data was physically stored. Rather, data sets were simply unordered, two-dimensional tables of data. To arrive at a workable way of deciding which pieces of data went into which table, Codd proposed "normal forms." To understand normal forms, we must first introduce the notion of "functional dependencies." After we understand functional dependences, the normal forms follow.

Checkpoint 1.2

1. What are the three main types of data models?
2. Which data model is mostly used today? Why?
3. What are some of the disadvantages of the hierarchical data model?
4. What are some of the disadvantages of the network data model?
5. How are all relationships (mainly the cardinalities) described in the hierarchical data model? How can these be a disadvantage of the hierarchical data model?
6. How are all relationships (mainly the cardinalities) described in the network data model? Would you treat these as advantages or disadvantages of the network data model? Discuss.
7. Why was Codd's promise of the relational model better?

Functional Dependencies

A functional dependency is a relationship of one attribute or field in a record to another. In a database, we often have the case where one field *defines* the other. For example, we can say that Social Security Number (SSN) defines a name. What does this mean? It means that if I have a database with SSNs and names, and if I know someone's SSN, then I can find their name. Further, because we used the word "defines," we are saying that for every SSN we will have one and only one name. We will say that we have *defined* name as being *functionally dependent* on SSN.

The idea of a functional dependency is to define one field as an anchor from which one can always find a single value for another field. As another example, suppose that a company assigned each employee a unique employee number. Each employee has a number and a name. Names might be the same for two different employees, but their employee numbers would always be different and unique because the company defined them that way. It would be inconsistent in the database if there were two occurrences of the same employee number with different names.

We write a functional dependency (FD) connection with an arrow:

$$\text{SSN} \quad \rightarrow \quad \text{Name}$$

or

$$\text{EmpNo} \quad \rightarrow \quad \text{Name.}$$

The expression SSN → Name is read "SSN defines Name" or "SSN implies Name."

Let us look at some sample data for the second FD.

EmpNo	Name
101	Kaitlyn
102	Brenda
103	Beryl
104	Fred
105	Fred

Wait a minute.... You have two people named Fred! Is this a problem with FDs? Not at all. You expect that Name will not be unique and it is commonplace for two people to have the same name. However, no two people have the same EmpNo and for each EmpNo, there is a Name.

Let us look at a more interesting example:

EmpNo	Job	Name
101	President	Kaitlyn
104	Programmer	Fred
103	Designer	Beryl
103	Programmer	Beryl

Is there a problem here? No. We have the FD that EmpNo → Name. This means that every time we find 104, we find the name, Fred. Just because something is on the left-hand side (LHS) of a FD, it does not imply that you have a key or that it will be unique in the database — the FD X → Y only means that for every occurrence of X you will get the same value of Y.

Let us now consider a new functional dependency in our example. Suppose that Job → Salary. In this database, everyone who holds a job title has the same salary. Again, adding an attribute to the previous example, we might see this:

EmpNo	Job	Name	Salary
101	President	Kaitlyn	50
104	Programmer	Fred	30
103	Designer	Beryl	35
103	Programmer	Beryl	30

Do we see a contradiction to our known FDs? No. Every time we find an EmpNo, we find the same Name; every time we find a Job title, we find the same Salary.

Let us now consider another example. We will go back to the SSN → Name example and add a couple more attributes.

SSN	Name	School	Location
101	David	Alabama	Tuscaloosa
102	Chrissy	MSU	Starkville
103	Kaitlyn	LSU	Baton Rouge
104	Stephanie	MSU	Starkville
105	Lindsay	Alabama	Tuscaloosa
106	Chloe	Alabama	Tuscaloosa

Here, we will define two FDs: SSN → Name and School → Location. Further, we will define this FD: SSN → School.

First, have we violated any FDs with our data? Because all SSNs are unique, there cannot be a FD violation of SSN → Name. Why? Because a FD X → Y says that given some value for X, you always get the same Y. Because the X's are unique, you will always get the same value. The same comment is true for SSN → School.

How about our second FD, School → Location? There are only three schools in the example and you may note that for every school, there is only one location, so no FD violation.

Now, we want to point out something interesting. If we define a functional dependency X → Y and we define a functional dependency Y → Z, then we know by inference that X → Z. Here, we defined SSN → School. We also defined School → Location, so we can *infer* that SSN → Location although that FD was not originally mentioned. The inference we have illustrated is called *the transitivity rule of FD inference*. Here is the transitivity rule restated:

$$\text{Given } X \rightarrow Y$$

$$\text{Given } Y \rightarrow Z$$

$$\text{Then } X \rightarrow Z$$

To see that the FD SSN → Location is true in our data, you can note that given any value of SSN, you always find a unique location for that person. Another way to demonstrate that the transitivity rule is true is to try to invent a row where it is not true and then see if you violate any of the defined FDs.

We defined these FD's:

Given: SSN → Name
        SSN → School
        School → Location

We are claiming by inference using the transitivity rule that SSN → Location. Suppose that we add another row with the same SSN and try a different location:

SSN	Name	School	Location
101	David	Alabama	Tuscaloosa
102	Chrissy	MSU	Starkville
103	Kaitlyn	LSU	Baton Rouge
104	Stephanie	MSU	Starkville
105	Lindsay	Alabama	Tuscaloosa
106	Chloe	Alabama	Tuscaloosa
106	Chloe	MSU	Starkville

Now, we have satisfied SSN → Name but violated SSN → Location. Can we do this? We have no value for School, but we know that if School = "Alabama" as defined by SSN → School, then we would have the following rows:

SSN	Name	School	Location
106	Chloe	Alabama	Tuscaloosa
106	Chloe	Alabama	Starkville

However, this is a problem. We cannot have Alabama and Starkville in the same row because we also defined School → Location. So in creating our counterexample, we came upon a contradiction to our defined FDs. Hence, the row with Alabama and Starkville is bogus. If you had tried to create a new location like this:

SSN	Name	School	Location
106	Chloe	Alabama	Tuscaloosa
106	Chloe	FSU	Tallahassee

You violate the FD, SSN → School — again, a bogus row was created. By being unable to provide a counterexample, you have demonstrated that the transitivity rule holds. You may prove the transitivity rule more formally (see Elmasri and Navathe, 2000, p. 479).

There are other inference rules for functional dependencies. We will state them and give an example, leaving formal proofs to the interested reader (see Elmasri and Navathe, 2000).

The Reflexive Rule

If X is a composite, composed of A and B, then X → A and X → B. Example: X = Name, City. Then we are saying that X → Name and X → City.
Example:

Name	City
David	Mobile
Kaitlyn	New Orleans
Chrissy	Baton Rouge

The rule, which seems quite obvious, says if I give you the combination `<Kaitlyn, New Orleans>`, what is this person's Name? What is this person's City? While this rule seems obvious enough, it is necessary to derive other functional dependencies.

The Augmentation Rule

If X → Y, then XZ → Y. You might call this rule, "more information is not really needed, but it doesn't hurt." Suppose we use the same data as before with Names and Cities, and define the FD Name → City. Now, suppose we add a column, `Shoe Size`:

Name	City	Shoe Size
David	Mobile	10
Kaitlyn	New Orleans	6
Chrissy	Baton Rouge	3

Now, I claim that because `Name → City`, that `Name+Shoe Size → City` (i.e., we augmented `Name` with `Shoe Size`). Will there be a contradiction here, ever? No, because we defined `Name → City`, `Name` plus more information will always identify the unique `City` for that individual. We can always add information to the LHS of an FD and still have the FD be true.

The Decomposition Rule

The decomposition rule says that if it is given that X → YZ (that is, X defines both Y and Z), then X → Y and X → Z. Again, an example:

Name	City	Shoe Size
David	Mobile	10
Kaitlyn	New Orleans	6
Chrissy	Baton Rouge	3

Suppose I define `Name → City, Shoe Size`. This means for every occurrence of `Name`, I have a unique value of `City` and a unique value of `Shoe Size`. The rule says that given `Name → City` and `Shoe Size` together, then `Name → City` and `Name → Shoe Size`. A partial proof using the reflexive rule would be:

```
Name → City, Shoe Size (given)
City, Shoe Size → City (by the reflexive rule)
Name → City            (using steps 1 and 2 and the transitivity rule)
```

The Union Rule

The union rule is the reverse of the decomposition rule in that if X → Y and X → Z, then X → YZ. The same example of `Name`, `City`, and

`Shoe Size` illustrates the rule. If we found independently or were given that `Name` → `City` and given that `Name` → `Show Size`, we can immediately write `Name` → `City, Shoe Size`. (Again, for further proofs, see Elmasri and Navathe, 2000, p. 480.)

You might be a little troubled with this example in that you may say that `Name` is not a reliable way of identifying `City`; `Names` might not be unique. You are correct in that `Names` may not ordinarily be unique, but note the language we are using. In this database, we *define* that `Name` → `City` and, hence, in this database are restricting `Name` to be unique by definition.

Keys and FDs

The main reason we identify the FDs and inference rules is to be able to find keys and develop normal forms for relational databases. In any relational table, we want to find out which, if any attribute(s), will identify the rest of the attributes. An attribute that will identify all the other attributes in row is called a "candidate key." A "key" means a "unique identifier" for a row of information. Hence, if an attribute or some combination of attributes will always identify all the other attributes in a row, it is a "candidate" to be "named" a key. To give an example, consider the following:

SSN	Name	School	Location
101	David	Alabama	Tuscaloosa
102	Chrissy	MSU	Starkville
103	Kaitlyn	LSU	Baton Rouge
104	Stephanie	MSU	Starkville
105	Lindsay	Alabama	Tuscaloosa
106	Chloe	Alabama	Tuscaloosa

Now suppose I define the following FDs:

$$SSN \rightarrow Name$$

$$SSN \rightarrow School$$

$$School \rightarrow Location$$

What I want is the fewest number of attributes I can find to identify all the rest — hopefully only one attribute. I know that `SSN` looks like a candidate, but can I rely on `SSN` to identify all the attributes? Put another way, can I show that `SSN` "defines" all attributes in the relation? I know that `SSN` defines `Name` and `School` because that is given. I know that I have the following transitive set of FDs:

$$SSN \rightarrow School$$

$$School \rightarrow Location$$

Therefore, by the transitive rule, I can say that SSN → Location. I have derived the three FDs I need. Adding the reflexive rule, I can then use the union rule:

SSN	→	Name	(given)
SSN	→	School	(given)
SSN	→	Location	(derived by the transitive rule)
SSN	→	SSN	(reflexive rule (obvious))
SSN	→	SSN, Name, School, Location	(union rule)

This says that given any SSN, I can find a unique value for each of the other fields for that SSN. SSN therefore is a candidate key for this relation. In FD theory, once we find all the FDs that an attribute defines, we have found the *closure* of the attribute(s). In our example, the closure of SSN is all the attributes in the relation. Finding a candidate key is the finding of a closure of an attribute or a set of attributes that defines all the other attributes.

Are there any other candidate keys? Of course! Remember the augmentation rule that tells us that because we have established the SSN as the key, we can augment SSN and form new candidate keys: SSN, Name is a candidate key. SSN, Location is a candidate key, etc. Because every row in a relation is unique, we always have at least one candidate key — the set of all the attributes.

Is School a candidate key? No. You do have the one FD that School → Location and you could work on this a bit, but you have no way to infer that School → SSN (and in fact with the data, you have a counter-example that shows that School does not define SSN).

Keys should be a minimal set of attributes whose closure is all the attributes in the relation — "minimal" in the sense that you want the fewest attributes on the LHS of the FD that you choose as a key. In our example, SSN will be minimal (one attribute), whose closure includes all the other attributes.

Once we have found a set of candidate keys (or perhaps only one as in this case), we designate one of the candidate keys as the primary key and move on to normal forms.

These FD rules are useful in developing Normal forms. Normal forms can be expressed in more than one way, but using FDs is arguably the easiest way to see this most fundamental relational database concept. E. Codd (1972) originally defined three normal forms: 1NF, 2NF, and 3NF.

Checkpoint 1.3

1. What are functional dependencies? Give examples.
2. What does the augmentative rule state? Give examples.
3. What does the decomposition rule state? Give examples.

A Brief Look at Normal Forms

In this section we briefly describe the first, second, and third normal forms.

First Normal Form (1NF)

The first normal form (1NF) requires that data in tables be two-dimensional — that there be no repeating groups in the rows. An example of a table not in 1NF is where there is an employee "record" such as:

```
Employee(name, address, {dependent name})
```

where {dependent name} infers that the attribute is repeated. Sample data for this record might be:

```
Smith, 123 4th St., {John, Mary, Paul, Sally}
Jones, 4 Moose Lane., {Edgar, Frank, Bob}
Adams, 88 Tiger Circle., {Kaitlyn, Alicia, Allison}
```

The problem with putting data in tables with repeating groups is that the table cannot be easily indexed or arranged so that the information in the repeating group can be found without searching each record individually. Relational people usually call a repeating group "nonatomic" (it has more than one value and can be broken apart).

Second Normal Form (2NF)

The second normal form (2NF) requires that data in tables depends on the whole key of the table. Partial dependencies are not allowed. An example:

```
Employee (name, job, salary, address)
```

where it takes a name + job combination (a concatenated key) to identify a salary, but address depends only on name. Some sample data:

Name	Job	Salary	Address
Smith	Welder	14.75	123 4th St
Smith	Programmer	24.50	123 4th St
Smith	Waiter	7.50	123 4th St
Jones	Programmer	26.50	4 Moose Lane
Jones	Bricklayer	34.50	4 Moose Lane
Adams	Analyst	28.50	88 Tiger Circle

Can you see the problem developing here? The address would be repeated for each occurrence of a name. This repeating is called *redundancy* and leads to *anomalies*. An anomaly means that there is a restriction on doing something due to the arrangement of the data. There are insertion anomalies, deletion anomalies, and update anomalies. The key of this table is Name + Job — this is clear because neither one is unique and it really takes both name and job to identify a salary. However, address depends only on the name, not the job; this is an example of a partial dependency. Address depends on only part of the key. An example of an insertion anomaly would be where one would want to insert a person into the table above, but the person to be inserted is not yet assigned a job. This cannot be done because a value would have to be known for the job attribute. Null values cannot be valid values for keys in relational databases (this is known as the entity-integrity constraint). An update anomaly would be where one of the employees changed his or her address. Three rows would have to be changed to accommodate this one change of address. An example of a delete anomaly would be that Adams quits, so Adams is lost, but then the information that the analyst is being paid $28.50 is also lost. Therefore, more related information than was previously anticipated is lost.

Third Normal Form (3NF)

The third normal form (3NF) requires that the data in tables depends on the primary key of the table. A classic example of non-3NF is:

```
Employee (name, address, project#, project-location)
```

Suppose that project-location means the location from which a project is controlled, and is defined by the project#. Some sample data will show the problem with this table:

Name	Address	Project#	Project-location
Smith	123 4th St	101	Memphis
Smith	123 4th St	102	Mobile
Jones	4 Moose Lane	101	Memphis

Note the redundancy in this table. Project 101 is located in Memphis; but every time a person is recorded as working on project 101, the fact that they work on a project that is controlled from Memphis is recorded again. The same anomalies — insert anomaly, update anomaly, and delete anomaly — are also present in this table.

To clear the database of anomalies and redundancies, databases must be normalized. The normalization process involves splitting the table into two or more tables (a decomposition). After tables are split apart (a process called decomposition), they can be reunited with an operation called a "join." There are three decompositions that would alleviate the normalization problems in our examples, as discussed below.

Examples of 1NF, 2NF, and 3NF

Example of Non-1NF to 1NF

Here, the repeating group is moved to a new table with the key of the table from which it came.

Non-1NF:

```
Smith, 123 4th St., {John, Mary, Paul, Sally}
Jones, 4 Moose Lane., {Edgar, Frank, Bob}
Adams, 88 Tiger Circle., {Kaitlyn, Alicia, Allison}
```

is decomposed into 1NF tables with no repeating groups:

1NF Tables:

EMPLOYEE table	
Name	*Address*
Smith	123 4th St
Jones	4 Moose Lane
Adams	88 Tiger Circle

DEPENDENT table	
DependentName	*EmployeeName*
John	Smith
Mary	Smith
Paul	Smith
Sally	Smith
Edgar	Jones
Frank	Jones
Kaitlyn	Adams
Alicia	Adams
Allison	Adams

In the EMPLOYEE table, Name is defined as a key — it uniquely identifies the rows. In the DEPENDENT table, the key is a combination (concatenation) of DependentName and EmployeeName. Neither the DependentName nor the EmployeeName is unique in the DEPENDENT table, and therefore both attributes are required to uniquely identify a row in the table. The Employee-Name in the DEPENDENT table is called a foreign key because it references a primary key, Name in another table, the EMPLOYEE table. Note that the original table could be reconstructed by combining these two tables by recording all the rows in the EMPLOYEE table and combining them with the corresponding rows in the EMPLOYEE table where the names were equal (an equi-join operation). Note that in the derived tables, there are no anomalies or unnecessary redundancies.

Example of Non-2NF to 2NF

Here, partial dependency is removed to a new table.

Non-2NF:

Name	Job	Salary	Address
Smith	Welder	14.75	123 4th St
Smith	Programmer	24.50	123 4th St
Smith	Waiter	7.50	123 4th St
Jones	Programmer	26.50	4 Moose Lane
Jones	Bricklayer	34.50	4 Moose Lane
Adams	Analyst	28.50	88 Tiger Circle

is decomposed into 2NF:

Name + Job table

NAME AND JOB		
Name	Job	Salary
Smith	Welder	14.75
Smith	Programmer	24.50
Smith	Waiter	7.50
Jones	Programmer	26.50
Jones	Bricklayer	34.50
Adams	Analyst	28.50

Name and Address (Employee info) table:

NAME AND ADDRESS	
Name	Address
Smith	123 4th St
Jones	4 Moose Lane
Adams	88 Tiger Circle

Again, note the removal of unnecessary redundancy and the amelioration removal of possible anomalies.

Example of Non-3NF to 3NF

Here, transitive dependency is removed to a new table.

Non-3NF:

Name	Address	Project#	Project-location
Smith	123 4th St	101	Memphis
Smith	123 4th St	102	Mobile
Jones	4 Moose Lane	101	Memphis

is decomposed into 3NF:

EMPLOYEE table:

EMPLOYEE		
Name	Address	Project#
Smith	123 4th St	101
Smith	123 4th St	102
Jones	4 Moose Lane	101

PROJECT table:

PROJECT	
Project#	Project-location
101	Memphis
102	Mobile
101	Memphis

Again observe the removal of the transitive dependency and the anomaly problem.

There are more esoteric normal forms, but most databases will be well constructed if they are normalized to the 3NF. The intent here is to show the general process and merits of normalization.

Checkpoint 1.4

1. Define 1NF, 2NF, and 3NF.
2. Why do databases have to be normalized?
3. Why should we avoid having attributes with multiple values or repeating groups?

Chapter Summary

This chapter was meant to serve as a background chapter for the reader. The chapter briefly described the software engineering process and how it is related to ER diagram design. Then the chapter gave a brief overview of the different data models, functional dependencies, and database normalization. The following chapters develop the ER design methodology in a step-by-step manner.

Chapter 1 Exercises

Example 1.1

If X → Y, can you say Y → X? Why or why not ?

Example 1.2

Decompose the following data into 1NF tables:

> Khanna, 123 4th St., Columbus, Ohio {Delhi University, Calcutta University, Ohio State}
> Ray, 4 Moose Lane, Pensacola, Florida {Zambia University, University of West Florida}
> Ali, 88 Tiger Circle, Gulf Breeze, Florida {University of South Alabama, University of West Florida}
> Sahni, 283 Penny Street, North Canton, Ohio {Wooster College, Mount Union College}

Example 1.3

Does the following data have to be decomposed?

Name	Address	City	State	Car	Color	Year
Smith	123 4th St.	Pensacola	FL	Mazda	Blue	2002
Smith	123 4th St.	Pensacola	FL	Nissan	Red	2001
Jones	4 Moose Lane	Santa Clive	CA	Lexus	Red	2000
Katie	5 Rain Circle	Fort Walton	FL	Taurus	White	2000

References

Armstrong, W., "Dependency Structures of Data Base Relationships," *Proceedings of the IFIP Congress*, 1974.

Chen, P.P., "The Entity Relationship Model — Toward a Unified View of Data," *ACM TODS 1*, No. 1, March 1976.

Codd, E., "A Relational Model for Large Shared Data Banks," *CACM*, 13, 6, June 1970.

Codd, E., Further Normalization of the Data Base Relational Model, in Rustin (1972).

Codd, E., "Recent Investigations in Relational Database System," *Proceedings of the IFIP Congress*, 1974.

Date, C., *An Introduction to Database Systems*, 6th ed., Addison-Wesley, Reading, MA, 1995.

Elmasri, R. and Navathe, S.B., *Fundamentals of Database Systems*, 3rd ed., Addison-Wesley, Reading, MA, 2000.

Maier, D., *The Theory of Relational Databases*, Computer Science Press, Rockville, MD, 1983.

Norman, R.J., *Object-Oriented Systems Analysis and Design*, Prentice Hall, Upper Saddle River, NJ, 1996.

Schach, S.R., *Classical and Object Oriented Software Engineering*, 4th ed., McGraw-Hill, New York, 1999.

Chapter 2

The Basic ER Diagram:
A Data Modeling Schema

Chapter Topics

This chapter begins by describing a data modeling approach and then introduces entity relationship (ER) diagrams. The concept of entities, attributes, relationships, and keys are introduced. The first three steps in an ER design methodology are developed. Step 1 begins by building a one-entity diagram. Step 2 concentrates on using structured English to describe a database. Step

3, the last section in this chapter, discusses mapping the ER diagram to a relational database. These concepts — the diagram, structured English, and mapping — will evolve together as the book progresses. At the end of the chapter we also begin a running case study, which will be continued at the ends of the subsequent chapters.

What Is a Data Modeling Schema?

A data modeling schema is a method that allows us to model or illustrate a database. This device is often in the form of a graphic diagram, but other means of communication are also desirable — non computer-people may or may not understand diagrams and graphics. The ER diagram (ERD) is a graphic tool that facilitates data modeling. The ERD is a subset of "semantic models" in a database. Semantic models refer to models that intend to elicit meaning from data. ERDs are not the only semantic modeling tools, but they are common and popular.

When we begin to discuss the contents of a database, the data model helps to decide which piece of data goes with which other piece of data on a conceptual level. An early concept in databases is to recognize that there are levels of abstraction that we can use in discussing databases. For example, if we were to discuss the filing of "names," we could discuss this:

> Abstractly, that is, "we will file names of people we know."

or

> Concretely, that is, "we will file first, middle, and last names (20 characters each) of people we know, so that we can retrieve the names in alphabetical order on last name, and we will put this data in a spreadsheet format on package x."

If a person is designing a database, the first step is to abstract and then refine the abstraction. The longer one stays away from the concrete details of logical models (relational, hierarchical, network) and physical realizations (fields [how many characters, the data type, etc.] and files [relative, spreadsheet]), the easier it is to change the model and to decide how the data will eventually be physically realized (stored). When we use the term "field" or "file," we will be referring to physical data as opposed to conceptual data.

Mapping is the process of choosing a logical model and then moving to a physical database file system from a conceptual model (the ER diagram). A physical file loaded with data is necessary to actually get data from a database. Mapping is the bridge between the design concept and physical reality. In this book we concentrate on the relational database model due to its ubiquitousness in contemporary database models.

What Is an Entity Relationship (ER) Diagram?

The ER diagram is a semantic data modeling tool that is used to accomplish the goal of abstractly describing or portraying data. Abstractly described data is called a ***conceptual model***. Our conceptual model will lead us to a "schema." A ***schema*** implies a permanent, fixed description of the structure of the data. Therefore, when we agree that we have captured the correct depiction of reality within our conceptual model, our ER diagram, we can call it a schema.

An ER diagram could also be used to document an existing database by reverse-engineering it; but in introducing the subject, we focus on the idea of using an ER diagram to model a to-be-created database and deal with reverse-engineering later.

Defining the Database — Some Definitions: Entity, Relationship, Attribute

As the name implies, an ER diagram models data as ***entities*** and ***relationships***, and entities have ***attributes***. An ***entity*** is a thing about which we store data, for example, a person, a bank account, a building. In the original presentation, Chen (1976) described an entity as a "thing which can be distinctly identified." So an entity can be a person, place, object, event, or concept about which we wish to store data.

The name for an entity must be one that represents a type or class of thing, not an instance. The name for an entity must be sufficiently generic but, at the same time, the name for an entity cannot be too generic. The name should also be able to accommodate changes "over time." For example, if we were modeling a business and the business made donuts, we might consider creating an entity called DONUT. But how long will it be before this business evolves into making more generic pastry? If it is anticipated that the business will involve pastry of all kinds rather than just donuts, perhaps it would be better to create an entity called PASTRY — it may be more applicable "over time."

Some examples of entities include:

- Examples of a person entity would be EMPLOYEE, VET, or STUDENT.
- Examples of a place entity would be STATE or COUNTRY.
- Examples of an object entity would be BUILDING, AUTO, or PRODUCT.
- Example of an event entity would be SALES, RETURNS, or REGISTRATION.
- Examples of a concept entity would be ACCOUNT or DEPARTMENT.

In older data processing circles, we might have referred to an entity as a record, but the term "record" is too physical and too confining; "record" gives us a mental picture of a physical thing and, in order to work at the conceptual level, we want to avoid device-oriented pictures for the moment. In a database context, it is unusual to store information about one entity, so we think of storing collections of data about entities — such collections are called ***entity sets***. Entity sets correspond to the concept of "files," but again, a file usually connotes a physical entity and hence we abstract the concept of the "file" (entity set) as well as the concept of a "record" (entity). As an example, suppose we have a company that has customers. You would imagine that the company had a customer entity set with individual customer entities in it.

An entity may be very broad (e.g., a person), or it may be narrowed by the application for which data is being prepared (like a student or a customer). *Broad* entities, which cover a whole class of objects, are sometimes called generalizations (e.g., person), and *narrower* entities are sometimes called specializations (e.g., student). In later diagrams (in this book) we will revisit generalizations and specializations; but for now, we will concern ourselves with an application level where there are no subgroups (specializations) or supergroups (generalizations) of entities.

When we speak of capturing data about a particular entity, we refer to this as an *instance*. An entity instance is a single occurrence of an entity. For example, if we create an entity called TOOL, and if we choose to record data about a screwdriver, then the screwdriver "record" is an instance of TOOL. Each instance of an entity must be uniquely identifiable so that each instance is separate and distinctly identifiable from all other instances of that type of entity. In a customer entity set, you might imagine that the company would assign a unique customer number, for example. This unique identifier is called a *key*.

A **relationship** is a link or association between entities. Relationships are usually denoted by verb phrases. We will begin by expanding the notion of an entity (in this chapter and the next), and then we will come back to the notion of a relationship (in Chapter 4) once we have established the concept of an entity.

An **attribute** is a property or characteristic for an entity. For example, an entity, AUTOMOBILE, may have attributes type, color, vehicle_id, etc.

A Beginning Methodology

Database modeling begins with a description of "what is to be stored." Such a description can come from anyone; we will call the describer the "user." For example, Ms. Smith of Acme Parts Company comes to you, asking that you design a database of parts for her company. Ms. Smith is the user. You are the database designer. What Ms. Smith tells you about the parts will be the database description.

As a starting point in dealing with a to-be-created database we will identify a central, "primary" entity — a category about which we will store data. For example, if we wanted to create a database about students and their environment, then one entity would be STUDENT (our characterization of an entity will always be in the singular). Having chosen one first primary entity, STUDENT, we will then search for information to be recorded about our STUDENT. This methodology of selecting one "primary" entity from a data description is our first step in drawing an ER diagram, and hence the beginning of the requirements phase of software engineering for our database.

Once the "primary" entity has been chosen, we then ask ourselves what information we want to record about our entity. In our STUDENT example, we add some details about the STUDENT — any details that will qualify, identify, classify, or express the state of the entity (in this case, the STUDENT entity). These details or contents of entities are called *attributes*.[1] Some example attributes of STUDENT would be the student's name, student number, major, address, etc. — information about the student.

ER Design Methodology

Step 1: Select one primary entity from the database requirements description and show attributes to be recorded for that entity.

"Requirements definition" is the first phase of software engineering where the systems analyst tries to find out what a user wants. In the case of a database, an information-oriented system, the user will want to store data. Now that we have chosen a primary entity and some attributes, our task will be to:

- Draw a diagram of our first-impression entity (our primary entity).
- Translate the diagram into English.
- Present the English (and the diagram) back to the user to see if we have it right and then progress from there.

The third step is called *"feedback"* in software engineering. The process of refining via feedback is a normal process in the requirements/specification phases. The feedback loop is essential in arriving at the reality of what one wants to depict from both the user and analyst viewpoints. First we will learn how to draw the entity and then we will present guidelines for converting our diagram into English.

Checkpoint 2.1

1. Of the following items, determine which could be an entity and state why: automobile, college class, student, name of student, book title, number of dependents.
2. Why are entities not called files or records?
3. What is mapping?
4. What are entity sets?
5. Why do we need Entity-Relationship Diagrams?
6. What are attributes? List attributes of the entities you found in question 1 (above).
7. What is a relationship?

---

[1] C. Date (1995) prefers the word "property" to "attribute" because it is more generic and because "attribute" is used in other contexts. We will use "attribute" because we believe it to be more commonly used.

A First "Entity-Only" ER Diagram: An Entity with Attributes

To recap our example, we have chosen an example with a "primary" entity from a student information database — the student. Again note that "a student" is something about which we want to store information (the definition of an entity). In this chapter, we do not concern ourselves with any other entities.

Let us think about some attributes of the entity STUDENT; that is, what are some attributes a student might have? A student has a name, an address, and an educational connection. We will call the educational connection a "school." We have picked three attributes for the entity STUDENT, and we have also chosen a generic label for each: name, address, school.

We begin our first venture into ER diagrams with a "Chen-like" model. Chen (1976) introduced the idea of the ER diagrams. He and others have improved the ER process over the years; and while there is no standard ERD model, the Chen-like model and variants thereof are common. After the "Chen-like" model, we introduce other models. We briefly discuss the "Barker/Oracle-like" model later (in Chapter 10). Chen-like models have the advantage that one does not need to know the underlying logical model to understand the design. Barker models and some other models require a full understanding of the relational model, and the diagrams are affected by relational concepts.

To begin, in the Chen-like model, we will do as Chen originally did and put the entities in boxes and the show attributes nearby. One way to depict attributes is to put them in circles or ovals appended to the boxes — see Figure 2.1 (top and middle). Figure 2.1 (bottom) is an alternative style of depicting attributes. The alternative attribute style (Figure 2.1, bottom) is not as descriptive, but it is more compact and can be used if Chen-like diagrams become cluttered.

There are several ways of depicting attributes. We have illustrated the "attribute in a circle" model (Chen-like model) because it is common and useful. Refer to Figure 2.2 for some alternate models for attributes. There are benefits to alternate forms for depicting attributes. The standard form of the Chen-like model with bubbles and boxes is good for conceptualizing; it is easily changed and very clear as to which attribute goes where. The concise form (Figure 2.1 [bottom] and other variants in Figure 2.2) is easily created from the standard form and is sometimes more useful for documentation when space is a concern.

Figure 2.1 (middle and bottom) shows an ER diagram with one entity, STUDENT, and three attributes: name, address, and school. If more attributes are added to our conceptual model, such as phone and major, they would be appended to the entity (here, STUDENT is the only entity we have), as can be seen in Figure 2.3.

More about Attributes

Attributes are characteristics of entities that provide descriptive details about the entities. There are several different kinds of attributes: simple or atomic,

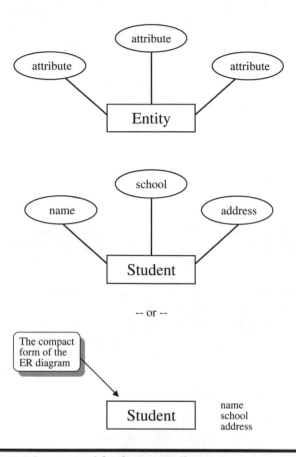

-- or --

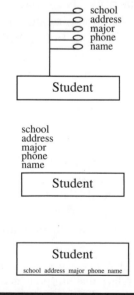

Figure 2.1   An ER Diagram with Three Attributes

Figure 2.2   An ER Diagram with One Entity and Five Attributes, Alternate Models (Batini, Ceri, Navathe)

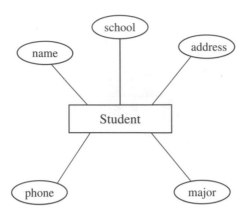

Figure 2.3   An ER Diagram with One Entity and Five Attributes

composite, multi-valued, and derived. The properties of an attribute are its name, description, format, and length, in addition to its atomiticity. Some attributes may be considered unique identifiers for an entity. This section also introduces the idea of a key attribute, a unique identifier for an entity.

The Simple or Atomic Attribute

Simple or atomic attributes cannot be further broken down or subdivided, hence the notion "atomic." One can examine the domain of values[2] of an attribute to elicit whether an attribute is simple or not. An example of a simple or atomic attribute would be Social Security number, where a person would be expected to have only one, undivided Social Security number.

Other tests of whether an attribute is simple or atomic will depend entirely on the circumstances that the database designer encounters — the desire of the "user" for which the database is being built. For example, we might treat a phone number attribute as simple in a particular database design, but in another scenario we may want to divide the phone number into two distinct parts, that is, the area code and the number. Another example of where the use of the attribute in the database will determine if the attribute is simple or atomic is — a birthdate attribute. If we are setting up a database for a veterinary hospital, it may make sense to break up a birthdate field into month, day, and year, because it will make a difference in treatment if a young animal is five days old versus if it is five months or five years old. Hence, in this case, birthdate would be a composite attribute. For a RACE HORSE database, however, it may not be necessary to break up a birthdate field into month/day/year, because all horses are dated only by the year in

---

[2] The "domain of values" is the set of values that a given attribute may take on. The domain consists of all the possible legal values that are permitted on an attribute. A data type is a broader term used to describe attributes, but "data type" includes the idea of what operations are allowable. Since database people are usually more concerned about storage and retrieval, database "data types" usually just focus on the "domain of values."

which they were born. In this latter case, birthdate, consisting of only the year, would be atomic.

If an attribute is non-atomic, it needs to be depicted as such on the ER diagram. The following sections deal with these more complicated, non-atomic attribute ideas — the composite attribute and the multi-valued attribute.

The Composite Attribute

A composite attribute, sometimes called a group attribute, is an attribute formed by combining or aggregating related attributes. The names chosen for composite attributes should be descriptive and general. The concept of "name" is adequate for a general description, but it may be desirable to be more specific about the parts of this attribute. Most data processing applications divide the name into component parts. Name, then, is called a **composite attribute** or an **aggregate** because it is usually composed of a first name, a last name, and a middle initial — sub-attributes, if you will. The way that composite attributes are shown in ER diagrams in the Chen-like model is illustrated in Figure 2.4. The sub-attributes, such as first name, middle initial, and last name, are called **simple**, **atomic,** or **elementary** attributes. The word "aggregate" is used in a different sense in some database query languages and to avoid confusion, but we will not call composite attributes "aggregates;" we will use the word "composite."

Once again, the test of whether or not an attribute will be composite will depend entirely on the circumstances that the database designer encounters — the desire of the "user" for which the database is being built. For example, in one database it may not be important to know exactly which city or state or zip code a person comes from, so an address attribute in that database

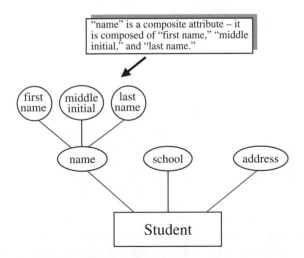

Figure 2.4   An ER Diagram with a Composite Attribute — name

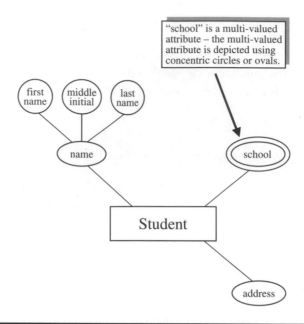

Figure 2.5   An ER Diagram with a Multi-Valued Attribute

may not be broken up into its component parts; it may just be called address. Whereas in another database, it may be important to know which city and state a person is from; so in this second database we would have to break up the address attribute into street address, city, state, and zip code, making the address attribute a composite attribute.

The Multi-Valued Attribute

Another type of non-simple attribute that has to be managed is called a ***multi-valued attribute***. The multi-valued attribute, as the name implies, may take on more than one value for a given occurrence of an entity. For example, the attribute school could easily be multi-valued if a person attends (or has attended, depending on the context of the database) more than one school. As a counter example, most people go by only one name and hence the grouping, name, is not multi-valued. The multi-valued attribute called school is depicted in Figure 2.5 (Chen-like model) as a double oval, which illustrates the situation where a database will store data about students who may have attended more than one school. Although we have chosen to illustrate school as a multi-valued attribute, we do not mean to imply that this will always be the case in all databases. In fact, the attribute, school, may well be singly valued in some databases. The idea of school may mean the current (or just-previous) school as opposed to all schools attended. If the subjects about whom we are storing data can attend only one school at a time (and that is what we want to depict), then the attribute, school, may well be a single-valued attribute.

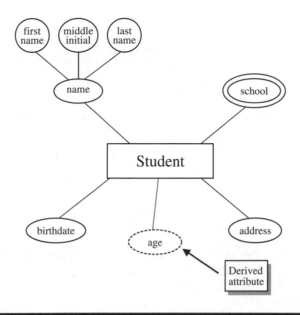

Figure 2.5A   An ER Diagram with a Derived Attribute — age

Once again, the test of single- versus multi-valued will depend entirely on the circumstances that the database designer encounters — the desire of the "user" for which the database is being built. It is recommended that if the sense of the database is that the attribute school means "current school," then the attribute should be called "current school" and illustrated as a single-valued attribute. In our example, we have a multi-valued attribute in Figure 2.5, so the sense of the diagram is that multiple schools can be recorded for each student.

The Derived Attribute

Derived attributes are attributes that the user may envision but may not be recorded per se. These derived attributes can be calculated from other data in the database. An example of a derived attribute would be an age that could be calculated once a student's birthdate is entered. In the Chen-like model, a derived attribute is shown in a dashed oval (as shown in Figure 2.5A).

Keys

The sense of a database is to store data for retrieval. An attribute that may be used to find a particular entity occurrence is called a **key**. As we model our database with the ER models, we may find that some attributes naturally seem to be keys. If an attribute can be thought of as a unique identifier for an entity, it is called a **candidate key**. When a candidate key is chosen to be **the** unique identifier, it becomes the **primary key** for the entity.

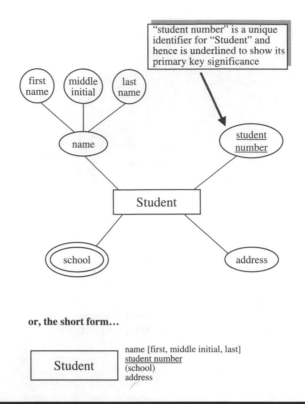

Figure 2.6   An ER Diagram with a Primary Key or Unique Identifier Attribute

As an example of keys, suppose we add an attribute called student number to our STUDENT entity example. We might well consider a student number to be a unique identifier for the entity — a candidate key because of uniqueness. Name is often unique, but not necessarily so. Members of the same class often share last names. Address may or may not be a unique identifier and hence is not a likely candidate key. Siblings that take classes together could easily have the same address. The point is that schools often choose to assign a unique student number to each student in order to be able to find student records — the sense of a key is to provide a unique way to find an entity instance (a particular record).

Some schools also choose to record a Social Security number (SSN) as an attribute. An SSN is also unique and hence a candidate key along with student number. If both SSN and student number were recorded, then the designer would have to choose which candidate would be the primary key. In our case, we choose not to record an SSN. The STUDENT entity with the unique identifier student number added as a <u>key</u>, is depicted in Figure 2.6.

In the Chen-like model, attributes that are ***unique identifiers*** (candidate keys) are usually underlined (as shown in Figure 2.6). A unique identifier can be an attribute or a combination of attributes. It is not necessary to choose which candidate key will be the primary key at this point, but one could do so. When there is only one candidate key, we will generally speak

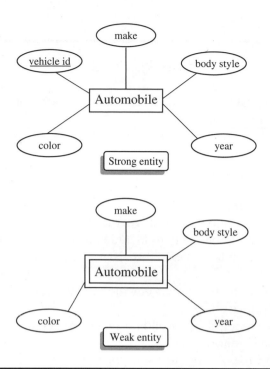

Figure 2.7   A Strong and a Weak AUTOMOBILE Entity

of it as the primary key, simply because it is obvious that the primary key is a candidate key. In Figure 2.6 we have also depicted the short form of the ER diagram (at the bottom) with composite attributes and multi-valued attributes as well as primary keys. The composite attributes are listed with its component parts, and the multi-valued attributes are enclosed in parentheses in the abbreviated form.

Finally, while on the subject of keys, we will have situations in the ER diagram (in the Chen-like model) where no key is obvious or intended. Entities that have at least one identified key can be called ***strong entities***. In Chen's (1976) original article, strong entities were called ***regular entities***. Some entities will be discovered which depend on other entities for their being (and hence their identification). Chen called those entities that rely on other entities for their existence, ***weak entities***.

We will often be able to recognize these weak entities because they may not have candidate keys, although the actual meaning of a weak entity is "one that depends on another for existence." As Chen did, we will follow the Chen-like notation and call such entities ***weak entities*** — weak because they will have to depend on some other entity to furnish a unique identifier to give the entity a reason to be recorded.

Although a weak entity may have a candidate key, it would not be a strong entity. We depict weak entities in the Chen-like ER diagrams with double boxes (see Figure 2.7). For now, we will concentrate on those entities that have keys, and later we will reconsider situations where no key is obvious.

Checkpoint 2.2

1. Describe the basic types of data representation schemas used in entity–relationship (ER) modeling.
2. What notation is used to diagrammatically show an entity in the Chen-like model?
3. How do we diagrammatically show attributes in the Chen-like model?
4. How do we show composite attributes in the Chen-like model?
5. Draw an entity representation for the entity "building" with the attributes building name, occupancy, and whether or not it has an elevator (yes/no).
6. Embellish the building entity to include the building superintendent's name (first, middle, and last). Does this have to be a composite attribute? Why or why not?
7. Embellish the building entity to include the address of the building, which will be the primary key.
8. Once again, embellish the building entity to include names (and only the names) of the janitorial staff.
9. Add a multi-valued attribute to the building entity.
10. How many attributes can an entity have?

English Description of the Entity

Now that we have an entity with attributes, we want to prepare the first feedback to the user — the English description. Users will not likely want to study the entity diagram but they well might want to hear what you, the analyst, think you heard. For an English description, we will use a "structured" English grammar and substitute the appropriate information from the entity diagram.

The Method

The guideline for the structured English for single entities is as follows.

Let *Entity* be the name of the entity and *att(j)* be the attributes. The order of the attributes is not important, so j = 1, 2, … is assigned arbitrarily. Suppose that there are *n* attributes so far. The generalized English equivalent of our diagram is:

The Entity

> This database records data about *Entity*. For each *Entity* in the database, we record *att(1)*, *att(2)*, *att(3)*, …, *att(n)*.

The Attributes

> For *atomic* attributes, a(j):
> > For each *Entity*, there always will be one and only one *att(j)* for each *Entity*. The value for *att(j)* will not be subdivided.
>
> For *composite* attributes, a(j):
> > For each *Entity*, we will record *att(j)*, which is composed of *x, y, z...*, *(x, y, z)* are the component parts of *att(j)*.
>
> For *multi-valued* attributes, a(j):
> > For each *Entity*, we will record *att(j)*'s. There may be more than one *att(j)* recorded for each *Entity*.
>
> For *derived* attributes, a(j):
> > For each *Entity*, there may exist *att(j)*'s, which will be derived from the database.

The Keys

For the key(s):

> (a) More than one candidate key (strong entity):
> > For each *Entity*, we will have the following candidate keys: *att(j), att(k)*, ..., [where *j, k* are candidate key attributes]
>
> (b) One candidate key (strong entity):
> > For each *Entity*, we will have the following primary key: *att(j)*
>
> (c) No candidate keys (weak entity):
> > For each *Entity1*, we do not assume that any attribute will be unique enough to identify individual entities without the accompanying reference to *Entity2*, the owner Entity.[3]
>
> (d) No candidate keys (intersecting entity):
> > For each *Intersecting Entity1*, we do not assume that any attribute will be unique enough to identify individual entities without the accompanying reference to *Entity2*, the owner Entity.

ER Design Methodology

Step 2: Use structured English for entities, attributes, and keys to describe the database that has been elicited.

Step 3: Show some sample data.

Sample data also helps describe the database as it is perceived.

---

[3] The details of the weak entity/strong entity relationship will become clearer as we introduce relationships in Chapter 3.

Examples

We will now revisit each of our figures and add an English description to each one. First, reconsider Figure 2.3. There are no multi-valued or composite attributes. *Entity* = STUDENT, *att(1)* = name, *att(2)* = school, etc. (j assigned arbitrarily). The English "translation" of the entity diagram using the above templates would be:

The Entity

> This database records data about STUDENTS. For each STUDENT in the database, we record a name, a school, an address, a phone number, and a major.

The Attributes

> For each name, there always will be one and only one name for each STUDENT. The value for name will not be subdivided.

> For each major, there always will be one and only one major for each STUDENT. The value for major will not be subdivided. (Note that in Figure 2.3 we did not divide name.)

> For each address, there always will be one and only one address for each STUDENT. The value for address will not be subdivided.

> For each school, there always will be one and only one school for each STUDENT. The value for school will not be subdivided.

> For each phone number, there always will be one and only one phone number for each STUDENT. The value for phone number will not be subdivided.

The Keys

> For each STUDENT, we do not assume that any attribute will be unique enough to identify individual entities. (Remember that we are describing Figure 2.3.)

Sample Data

In addition to the above descriptions, some sample data is often very helpful in showing the user what you have proposed:

STUDENT				
name	*major*	*address*	*school*	*phone number*
Smith	Cosc	123 4th St	St. Helens	222–2222
Jones	Acct	222 2nd St	PS 123	333–3333
Saha	Eng	284 3rd St	Canton	345–3546
Kapoor	Math	20 Living Cr	High	435–4534

Now consider Figure 2.4. This figure has a composite attribute — name. The English "translation" of this entity diagram would be as follows:

The Entity

> This database records data about STUDENTS. For each STUDENT in the database, we record a name, a school, and an address.

The Attributes

> For each name, there always will be one and only one name for each STUDENT. The value for name will be subdivided into a first name, a last name, and a middle initial.

> For each address, there always will be one and only one address for each STUDENT. The value for address will not be subdivided.

> For each school, there will be one and only one school for each STUDENT. The value of the school will not be subdivided.

The Keys

> For each STUDENT, we do not assume that any attribute will be unique enough to identify individual entities.

Sample Data

STUDENT				
name.first	*name.last*	*name.mi*	*school*	*address*
Richard	Earp	W	U. Alabama	222 2nd St
Boris	Backer		Heidleburg	333 Dreistrasse
Helga	Hogan	H	U. Hoover	88 Half Moon Ave
Arpan	Bagui	K	Northern School	33 Bloom Ave
Hema	Malini		South Bend	100 Livingstone

Next consider Figure 2.5. This figure has a composite as well as a multi-valued attribute. The English "translation" of this entity diagram would be as follows:

The Entity

This database records data about STUDENTS. For each STUDENT in the database, we record a name, a school, and an address.

The Attributes

For each name, there always will be one and only one name for each STUDENT. The value for name will be subdivided into a first name, a last name, and a middle initial.

For each address, there always will be one and only one address for each STUDENT. The value for address will not be subdivided.

For each STUDENT, we will record schools. There may be more than one school recorded for each student.

The Keys

For each STUDENT, we do not assume that any attribute will be unique enough to identify individual entities.

Sample Data

		STUDENT		
name.first	*name.last*	*name.mi*	*school*	*address*
Richard	Earp	W	U. Alabama, Mountain	222 2nd St
Boris	Backer		Heidleburg, Volcano	333 Dreistrasse
Helga	Hogan	H	U. Hoover, St. Helens	88 Half Moon Ave
Arpan	Bagui	K	Northern School	33 Bloom Ave
Hema	Malini		South Bend	100 Livingstone

Consider Figure 2.6. This figure has a composite, multi-valued, as well as key attribute. The English "translation" of this entity diagram would be as follows:

The Entity

This database records data about STUDENTS. For each STUDENT in the database, we record a name, schools, an address, and a student number.

The Attributes

For each name, there always will be one and only one name for each STUDENT. The value for name will be subdivided into a first name, a last name, and a middle initial.

For each address, there always will be one and only one address for each STUDENT. The value for address will not be subdivided.

For each STUDENT, we will record schools. There may be more than one school recorded for each student.

The Keys

For each STUDENT, we will assume that there is an attribute — student number — that will be unique enough to identify individual entities.

Finally, consider Figure 2.7 (top). This figure shows a strong entity. We will combine the grammar a little to keep the methodology from being overly repetitive. The English "translation" of this entity diagram would be as follows:

The Entity

This database records data about AUTOMOBILEs. For each AUTOMOBILE in the database, we record a make, body style, year, color, and vehicle-id.

The Attributes

Each AUTOMOBILE will have one and only one make, body style, year, color, and vehicle-id. None of these attributes will be subdivided.

The Keys

For each AUTOMOBILE, we assume that attribute vehicle-id will be unique enough to identify individual entities.

Figure 2.7 (bottom) shows a weak entity. The only difference between the strong and weak entity description involves the key phrase, which may not exist in the weak entity.

Figure 2.8 shows a relationship between two entities, an AUTOMOBILE and a STUDENT. The concept of relationships is discussed in more detail in Chapter 4.

Our methodology has evolved as follows:

ER Design Methodology

Step 1: Select one primary entity from the database requirements description and show attributes to be recorded for that entity. Label key if appropriate.

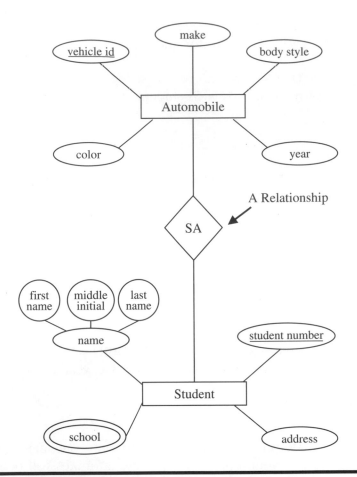

Figure 2.8   An ER Diagram of the STUDENT-AUTOMOBILE Database

Step 2: Use structured English for entities, attributes, and keys to describe the database that has been elicited.

Step 3: Show some data.

Mapping the Entity Diagram to a Relational Database

Having illustrated the ideas of the entity and the attribute, we now turn to a semi-physical realization of the concepts. We say "semi-physical" because we are really not concerned with the actual physical file that is stored on a disk, but rather we are concerned with placing data into relational tables that we will visualize as a physical organization of data. Basically, a relational database is a database of two-dimensional tables called "relations." The tables are composed of rows and columns. The rows are often called ***tuples*** and the columns, ***attributes***. In relational databases, all attributes (table columns) must be atomic and keys must not be null. In addition, in relational databases, the actual physical location of the data on a disk is not usually necessary to know.

The process of converting an ER diagram into a database is called ***mapping***. We concern ourselves only with the relational model and hence, as the chapters in this book develop, we will consider mapping rules to map ER diagrams into relational databases.

We start with a rule to map strong entities:

> **M1 — for strong entities: develop a new table (relation) for each strong entity and make the indicated key of the strong entity the primary key of the table. If more than one candidate key is indicated on the ER diagram, choose one for the primary key.**

Next, we must map the attributes into the strong entity. Mapping rules are different for atomic attributes, composite attributes, and multi-valued attributes. First, we present the mapping rule for mapping atomic attributes:

> **M1a — mapping atomic attributes from an entity — for entities with atomic attributes: map entities to a table by forming columns for the atomic attributes.[4]**

A relational database realization of the ER diagram in Figure 2.3 with some data would look like this:

		STUDENT		
name	phone	school	address	major
Jones	932–5100	U. Alabama	123 4th St	Chemistry
Smith	932–5101	U. Mississippi	123 5th St	Math
Adams	932–5102	LSU	123 6th St	Agriculture
Sumon	435–0997	UWF	11000 Univ	Comp Sc
Mala	877–0982	Mount Union	North Canton	History

The entity name, STUDENT, would be the name of the relation (table). The attributes in the diagram become the column headings. The actual table with data, a realization of a relation, is provided as an example of the type of data you might expect from such a relation. The ordering of the columns is irrelevant to relational database as long as once the ordering is chosen, we stay with it.

What about the composite and multi-valued attributes? As mentioned above, it is an axiom of relational databases that all columns be atomic. If we have a non-atomic attribute in our diagram, we have to make it atomic for mapping to the relational database. For composite attributes, we achieve atomicity by recording only the component parts of the attribute.

---

[4] These mapping rules are adapted from Elmasri and Navathe (2000).

Our next mapping rule concerns composite attributes:

M1b – for entities with composite attributes: map entities to a table by forming columns from the elementary (atomic) parts of the composite attributes.

Refer to Figure 2.4. A relational database, which corresponds to the entity diagram in Figure 2.4, would look like this:

		STUDENT		
name.first	*name.last*	*name.mi*	*school*	*address*
Richard	Earp	W	U. Alabama	222 2nd St
Boris	Backer		Heidleburg	333 Dreistrasse
Helga	Hogan	H	U. Hoover	88 Half Moon Ave
Arpan	Bagui	K	Northern School	33 Bloom Ave
Hema	Malini		South Bend	100 Livingstone

Multi-valued attributes were depicted in Figure 2.5. In this entity diagram, our STUDENT entity had a composite attribute, name, and a multi-valued attribute, school. This means that a student may have more than one school recorded for his (or her) row. Data that would be represented by this diagram might look like this (to illustrate our point with multi-valued attributes, we are only showing the name, the address, and the schools they attended):

	STUDENT	
name	*address*	*school*
Smith	123 4th St	St. Helens, Mountain, Volcano
Jones	222 2nd St	Manatee U, Everglades High
Sudip	887 Mirabelle	PCA, Pensacola High, UWF
Pradeep	248 Shillingford	Cuttington, UT

Note that this is not a relational table because school is not atomic.

A mapping rule for multi-valued attributes would be this:

M1c — for multi-valued attributes: form a separate table for the multi-valued attribute. Record a row for each value of the multi-valued attribute, together with the key from the original table. The key of the new table will be the concatenation of the multi-valued attribute plus the key of the owner entity. Remove the multi-valued attribute from the original table.

Now suppose that the above example had name as a key. It would be mapped into two relations: a relation with the multi-valued attribute, and a resulting relation with the multi-valued attribute excised.

Relation with the Multi-Valued Attribute:

Name–School	
name	*school*
Smith	St. Helens
Smith	Mountain
Smith	Volcano
Jones	Manatee U
Jones	Everglades High
Sudip	PCA
Sudip	Pensacola High
Sudip	UWF
Pradeep	Cuttington
Pradeep	UT

Resulting Relation with the Multi-Valued Attribute Excised:

STUDENT	
name	*address*
Smith	123 4th St
Jones	222 2nd St
Sudip	887 Mirabelle
Pradeep	248 Shillingford

With no key, the mapping rule remains the same except that, instead of "together with the key, …" we would say "together with the atomic attributes..." In relational databases, every row of a table contains atomic attributes. Also, every row is unique. Therefore, a candidate key in any table is always *all* of the attributes. Usually, a subset of "all of the attributes" can be found to be a key; but because no two rows are ever the same, we would say that one candidate key is the collection of all attributes.

If the name or address attributes were not considered unique, then the resulting relation would be:

STUDENT		
name	*address*	*school*
Smith	123 4th Street	St. Helens
Smith	123 4th Street	Mountain
Smith	123 4th Street	Volcano
Jones	222 2nd St	Manatee U
Jones	222 2nd St	Everglades High
Sudip	887 Mirabelle	PCA
Sudip	887 Mirabelle	Pensacola High
Sudip	887 Mirabelle	UWF
Pradeep	248 Shillingford	Cuttington
Pradeep	248 Shillingford	UT

Note that rule M1c is an application of the non-1NF to 1NF transformation discussed in Chapter 1.

Checkpoint 2.3

1. How do you map multi-valued attributes?
2. How do you map composite attributes?
3. What is a unique identifier? Is it a candidate key? Is it "the" primary key? Discuss.

Chapter Summary

The main focus in this chapter was on developing the concept of the entity and developing a one-entity diagram (using the Chen-like model). The concept of attributes was also discussed, and the final section focused on how a one-entity diagram could be mapped to a relational database. The grammar for a one-entity diagram and its attributes was also developed. This grammar will be further developed in subsequent chapters. Chapter 3 discusses developing a second entity, and the relationship between this second entity and the "primary entity."

Chapter 2 Exercises

[*Note:* You should filter out and clarify the assumptions you made when you report your work.]

Exercise 2.1

You want to create a database about businesses. Each business will have a name, an address, the business phone number, the owner's phone number, and the first names of the employees who work at the business. Draw the ER diagram using the Chen-like model, and then write the English description for your diagrams. Compare the English to your diagrams, and state any assumptions you made when drawing the diagrams. Map your diagrams to a relational database.

Which attributes would you consider composite attributes in this database? Which attributes would you consider multi-valued attributes in this database? Could there be any derived attributes? What would be good keys?

Exercise 2.2

You want to create a database about the books on your shelf. Each book has authors (assume last name only is needed), title, publisher, courses used in (course number only). Draw the ER diagram using the Chen-like model, and then write out the English description for your diagrams. Compare the English to your diagrams and state any assumptions you made when drawing the diagrams.

Which attributes would you consider composite attributes in this database? Which attributes would you consider multi-valued attributes in this database? Could there be any derived attributes? What would be good keys? Map your diagram to a relational database.

References

Batini, C., Ceri, S., and Navathe, S.B., *Conceptual Database Design*, Benjamin Cummings, Redwood City, CA, 1992.

Chen, P.P., "The Entity Relationship Model — Toward a Unified View of Data," *ACM Transactions on Database Systems,* 1(1), 9–37, March 1976.

Chen, P.P., "The Entity-Relationship Model: A Basis for the Enterprise View of Data," *Proceedings IFIPS NCC 46,* No. 46, 76–84, 1977.

Codd, E., *Relational Model for Data Management – Version 2*, Addison-Wesley, Reading, MA, 1990.

Date, C.J., *An Introduction to Database Systems*, 5th ed., Addison-Wesley, Reading, MA, 1995.

Earp, R. and Bagui, S., "Building an Entity Relationship Diagram: A Software Engineering Approach," *Database Management*, Auerbach Publications, Boca Raton, FL, 22-10-41, 1–16, December 2000.

Elmasri, R. and Navathe, S.B., *Fundamentals of Database Systems*, 3rd ed., Addison-Wesley, Reading, MA, 2000.

McFadden, F.R. and Hoffer, J.A., *Modern Database Management,* 4th ed., Benjamin Cummings, Menlo Park, CA, 1994.

Navathe, S. and Cheng, A., "A Methodology for Database Schema Mapping from Extended Entity Relationship Models into the Hierarchical Model," *The Entity-Relationship Approach to Software Engineering*, G.C. Davis et al., Eds., Elsevier, North-Holland, Amsterdam, 1983.

Scheuermann, P., Scheffner, G., and Weber, H., "Abstraction Capabilities and Invariant Properties Modeling within the Entity-Relationship Approach," *Entity-Relationship Approach to System Analysis and Design*, P. Chen, Ed., Elsevier, North-Holland, Amsterdam, 121–140, 1980.

Teorey, T.J., Yang, D., and Fry, J.P., "A Logical Design Methodology for Relational Databases Using the Extended Entity-Relationship Model," *ACM Computing Surveys,* 18(2), 197–222, June 1986.

Valacich, J.S., George, J.F., and Hoffer, J.A., *Essentials of Systems Analysis and Design,* Prentice Hall, Upper Saddle River, NJ, 2001.

Case Study: West Florida Mall

A new mall, West Florida Mall, just had its grand opening three months ago in Pensacola, Florida. This new mall is attracting a lot of customers and stores. West Florida Mall, which is part of a series of malls owned by a parent company, now needs a database to keep track of the management of the mall in terms of keeping track of all its stores as well as the owners and workers of the stores. Before we build a database for this system of malls, the first step will be to design an ER diagram for the mall owner. We gathered the following initial user specifications about the malls, with which we can start creating our the ER diagram:

- We need to record information about the mall and each store in the mall. We will need to record the mall's name and address. A mall, at any point in time, must contain one or more stores.
- For each store, we will need to keep the following information: store number (which will be unique), the name of the store, the location of the store (room number), departments, the owner of the store, and manager of the store. Each store may have more than one department, and each department is managed by a manager. Each store will have only one store manager. Each store is owned by only one owner. Each store is located in one and only one mall.
- A store manager can manage only one store. We have to record information on the store manager: the name, social security number, which store he or she is working for, and salary.
- The store owner is a person. We have to record information about the store owner, such as name, social security number, address, and office phone number. A store owner has to own at least one store, and may own more than one store.

Developing the Case Study

As per step 1 in designing the ER diagram, we must select our primary entity, and then the attributes for our primary entity (step 1 is shown below):

Step 1: Select one primary entity from the database requirements description and show attributes to be recorded for that entity.

We will choose MALL as our primary entity. For the MALL we will record a name, an address, and store_names.

Our next step will be to translate the diagram into English.

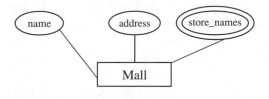

Figure 2.9 The MALL Entity

Step 2: Use structured English for entities, attributes, and keys to describe the database that has been elicited.

The Entity

This database records data about a MALL. For each MALL in the database, we record a name, an address, and store_names.

The Attributes for MALL

For each name, there always will be one and only one name for the mall. The value for name will not be subdivided.

For each address, there always will be one and only one address for the mall. The value for address will not be subdivided.

For each MALL, we will record store_names. There may be more than one store_name recorded for each MALL. The value of each store_name will not be subdivided.

The Keys

For each MALL, we will assume that the mall name (name) will be unique.

The MALL entity is shown in Figure 2.9. So far for this case study, we selected one primary entity (MALL), showed its known attributes, and used structured English to describe the entity and its attributes. Next, we will map this entity diagram to a relational database.

Mapping the Entity to a Relational Database

MALL is a strong entity, so using mapping rule M1 which states:

M1 — for strong entities: develop a new table for each strong entity and make the indicated key of the strong entity the primary key of the table. If more than one candidate key is indicated on the ER diagram, choose one for the primary key.

We will develop a new relation for the entity MALL (as shown in Figure 2.9), and name will be our primary key. Data that would be represented by Figure 2.9 might look like the following:

	MALL	
name	address	store_names
West Florida Mall	N Davis Hwy, Pensacola, FL	Penney's, Sears, Dollar Store, Rex
Cordova Mall	9th Avenue, Pensacola, FL	Dillards, Parisian, Circuit City, Radio Shack
Navy Mall	Navy Blvd, Pensacola, FL	Belks, Wards, Pearle Vision, McRaes, Sears
BelAir Mall	10th Avenue, Mobile, AL	Dillards, Sears, Penney's, Best Buy, Pizza Hut

We can see that MALL has a multi-valued attribute, store_names. This does not make the above table a relational table because store_names is not atomic — it is multi-valued. For multi-valued attributes, the mapping rule is:

M1c. For multi-valued attributes, form a separate table for the multi-valued attribute. Record a row for each value of the multi-valued attribute together with the key from the original table. Remove the multi-valued attribute from the original table.

Using this mapping rule, the above data would be mapped to two relations: a relation with the multi-valued attribute and a relation with the multi-valued attribute excised.

Relation with the Multi-Valued Attribute:

MALL–Store	
name	store_name
West Florida Mall	Penney's
West Florida Mall	Sears
West Florida Mall	Dollar Store
West Florida Mall	Rex
Cordova Mall	Dillards
Cordova Mall	Parisian
Cordova Mall	Circuit City
Cordova Mall	Radio Shack
Navy Mall	Belks
Navy Mall	Wards
Navy Mall	Pearle Vision

MALL–Store	
name	*store_name*
Navy Mall	McRaes
Navy Mall	Sears
BelAir Mall	Dillards
BelAir Mall	Sears
BelAir Mall	Penney's
BelAir Mall	Best Buy
Bel Air Mall	Pizza Hut

Relation with the Multi-Valued Attribute Excised

MALL	
name	*address*
West Florida Mall	N Davis Hwy, Pensacola, FL
Cordova Mall	9th Avenue, Pensacola, FL
Navy Mall	Navy Blvd, Pensacola, FL
BelAir Mall	10th Avenue, Mobile, AL

Our relational database maps to:

[*Note:* The primary keys are underlined.]

MALL–Store

name	store_name

MALL

name	address

This case study will be continued at the end of Chapter 3.

Chapter 3

Beyond the First Entity Diagram

Chapter Topics

Now that we have devised a method for drawing, interpreting, and refining one primary entity, we need to move to more complex databases. To progress from here, we continue with our primary entity and look for other information that would be associated with (related to) that entity.

The first technique employed in this chapter is methodical; we test our primary entity to see whether or not our "attributes" should be entities themselves. We will then look for other pieces of information in our description, add them to (1) an existing entity and examine the existing ER diagram, or (2) create a new entity directly. After creating the new entities, we look to see what kind of relationships exist between the two entities. This chapter develops steps 3, 4, and 5 of the ER design methodology presented in this book. Step 3 examines the attributes of the primary entity, step 4 discusses what to do if another entity is needed, and step 5 discusses developing the relationship between the two entities.

Although the concept of relationships is introduced in this chapter, we do not include any new mapping rules in this chapter because mapping rules can be better understood after the development of structural constraints on relationships, which is discussed in Chapter 4. At the end of this chapter, we continue with the case study that began in Chapter 2.

Examining an Entity — Changing an Attribute to an Entity

Consider Figure 3.1. In this figure, we have a student with the following attributes: name (a composite attribute), student number (an atomic attribute and key), schools (a multi-valued attribute). Suppose that during our first session with the user, we show the diagram, the English, and the sample data, and the user says, "Wait, I want to record all schools that a student attended and I want to record not only the name of the school, but also the location (city and state) and school type (community college, university, high school, etc.)."

What the user just told us was that the attribute, schools, should really be an entity. Remember that the definition of entity was something about which we wanted to record information. Our original thought was that we were recording schools attended, but now we are told that we want to record information about the schools. The first indicator that an attribute should be considered an entity is that we need to store information about the attribute. What we do then is migrate from Figure 3.1 to Figure 3.2. In Figure 3.2, SCHOOL is now an entity all by itself, so now we have two separate entities: SCHOOL and STUDENT. The next step is to define a relationship between the two entities. We assume school-name to be unique and choose the name of the school as the key for the entity, SCHOOL.

Defining a Relationship for Our New Entity

Databases are designed to store related data. For example, it would ordinarily make no sense to record data about students and foreign currencies or about

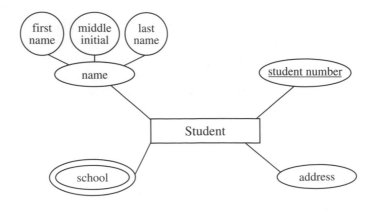

Figure 3.1   A STUDENT Entity with a Multi-Valued Attribute

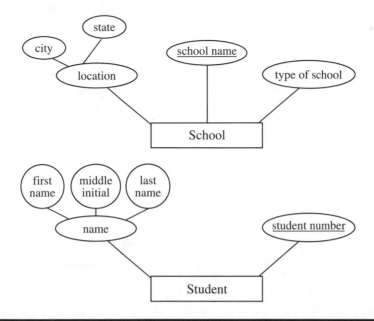

Figure 3.2   Two ER Diagrams: One of STUDENT and One of SCHOOL

airline flights and employees at a tennis ball factory in the same database. These concepts are not related. In a database we should be creating a collection of related data. Following our method, we clearly have a situation in which an attribute was part of an entity (school was considered "part of" student), but now school has become an entity all by itself. What we have to do now is relate the SCHOOL entity to the STUDENT entity.

In Figure 3.2, we have two entities but they appear as though they are independent. To make the SCHOOL entity and the STUDENT entity function as a database, we have to add something — the relationship that the entity SCHOOL has to the entity STUDENT.

A relationship in an ER diagram is a connection between two or more entities, or between one entity and itself. The latter kind of relationship, between one entity and itself, is known as a *recursive* relationship, which we will discuss later (in Chapter 6). A relationship name is usually a verb or verb phrase that denotes the connection between entities. Once we understand how the relationship is denoted, we will have a "tool" to draw a database description in the form of an ER diagram.

In the Chen-like model, a relationship is depicted by a diamond on the line that joins the two entities together, as shown in Figure 3.3.

In Figure 3.3, the relationship is depicted as attend. The sense of the relationship is that of a verb connecting two nouns (entities). All relationships are two-way. As we will see, it is necessary to state all relationships from both directions. For example, in the Chen-like model, we would informally say, "STUDENTS attend SCHOOLS" or "SCHOOLS are attended by STUDENTS."

The degree of a relationship refers to the number of entities that participate in the relationship. In Figure 3.3, two entities are participating in the relationship attend, so this is called a binary relationship.

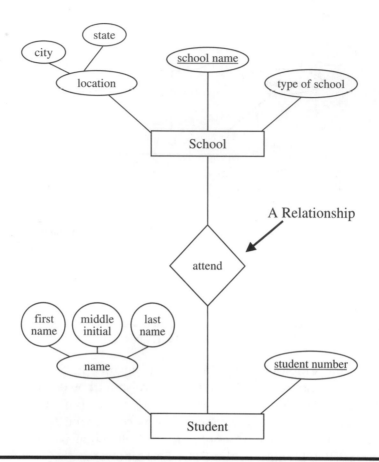

Figure 3.3   The STUDENT Entity with a Relationship to the SCHOOL Entity

We now have a tool to "draw" a database description in the form of an ER (entity relationship) diagram. The sense of our diagrams is that we record information about x and about y (x and y are entities) and then tell what the relationship of x to y is.

Our growing and amended methodology is now this:

ER Design Methodology

Step 1: Select one, primary entity from the database requirements description and show attributes to be recorded for that entity. Label keys if appropriate and show some sample data.

Step 2: Use structured English for entities, attributes, and keys to describe the database that has been elicited.

Step 3: Examine attributes in the primary entity (possibly with user assistance) to find out if information about one of the entities is to be recorded.

Step 3a: If information about an attribute is needed, then make the attribute an entity, and then

Step 3b: Define the relationship back to the original entity.

Step 4: Show some sample data.

A Preliminary Grammar for the ER Diagrams

Chapter 2 outlined a grammar to describe an entity. Now that we have added a relationship to our diagram, we need to embellish our English description of the proposed database. We also want to show the user some sample data to solidify the understanding of the path we are taking. We want to add the following to our list of grammatical expressions.

For each relationship, we add the following comment (in loose English [for now]):

> A(n) Entity1 Relationship Entity2 (active voice) and a(n) Entity2 Relationship Entity1 (passive voice).

Here, we would say (in addition to the entity/attribute descriptions from Chapter 2):

The Relation

> STUDENTS attend SCHOOLS and SCHOOLS are attended by STUDENTS.

Sometimes a singular description will fit the problem better and, if so, you may use it:

> A STUDENT attends SCHOOLS and a SCHOOL is attended by STUDENTS.

The user may be the ultimate judge of the appropriateness of the expression we use, but we will be adding to this grammar soon. As an exercise, you will be asked to provide complete descriptions of the ER diagrams in Figure 3.3, with all entities, attributes, keys, and relationships.

Defining a Second Entity

Having examined the original primary entity for suspicious attributes, we can now begin to add more data. Let us look at different database information from the user. Let us suppose this time that we have the following additional description. We want to record information about students — their name and student numbers. In addition to information about students, we want to record information about their automobiles. We want to record the vehicle identification number, the make of the car, body style, color, and the year of the model.

Let us further suppose that we made the decision to choose student as the primary entity and we want to add the automobile information.

The automobile is clearly an entity in that it is something about which we want to record information. If we add the automobile into the database, we could have included it as in step 1 of our methodology by adding an attribute called automobile, only later to perform step 3 of the methodology and migrate it and school to the status of entities. The depiction of automobile as an attribute of the student entity is shown in Figure 3.4 (in the Chen-like model). [We ignore the SCHOOL entity for the moment].

If we added the attribute, automobile, to the entity, STUDENT, and then recognized that automobile should have been an entity, we would create the AUTOMOBILE entity and then add the relationship to the model. (Note that Figure 3.4 would actually be sufficient if the user did not want to store information about the automobiles themselves.)

Of course, we could have recognized that the automobile attribute was going to be an entity all along, and simply recorded it as such in our diagram in the first place. By recognizing AUTOMOBILE as an entity, we would draw the two entities, STUDENT and AUTOMOBILE, and then look for a relationship between the two. Either way, we would end up with Figure 3.5, with two entities, STUDENT and AUTOMOBILE, and some relationship between the two.

In the Chen-like notation, we now choose some verb to describe the relationship between the two entities (STUDENT and AUTOMOBILE) — in

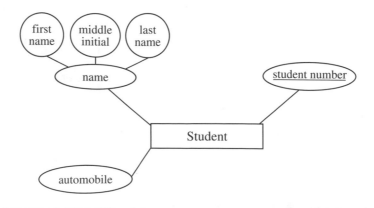

Figure 3.4   A STUDENT Entity with an Attribute Called AUTOMOBILE

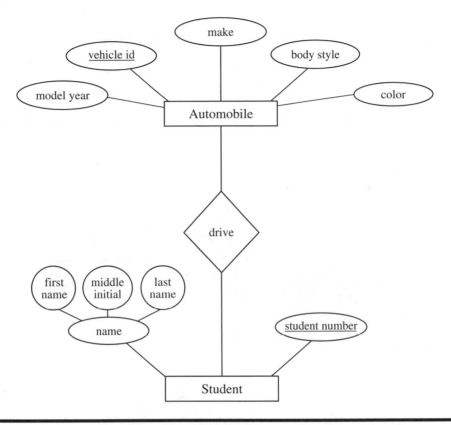

Figure 3.5   An ER Diagram of the STUDENT–AUTOMOBILE Database

this case, we choose drive (shown in the diamond). Note that later the user may choose to identify the relationship as something else; but with no other information, we assume the user means that students drive automobiles. Other candidates for a relationship between the STUDENT and AUTOMOBILE entities might be "register," "own," etc. This relationship between two entities is known as a binary relationship.

Relationships in ER diagrams are usually given names that depict how the entities are related. Sometimes, a relationship is difficult to describe (or unknown), and in this case a two-letter code for the relationship is used. This two-letter relationship is shown in Figure 3.6 where we have given the relationship the name "SA" to indicate that we understand that a relationship exists, but we are not clear on exactly what to call it (SA = STUDENT–AUTO-MOBILE). Of course, if we were confident of "drive" as the relationship, we would use "drive."

The English description of the entities and relationships implies that entities are nouns and relationships are verbs. Using the drive relationship (as shown in Figure 3.6), Students (N) drive (V) automobiles (N). If the "unknown" relationship is really unknown, we might say that Students (N) are related to (V) automobiles (N). Chapter 4 develops this English description as well as the relationship part of the diagram more fully.

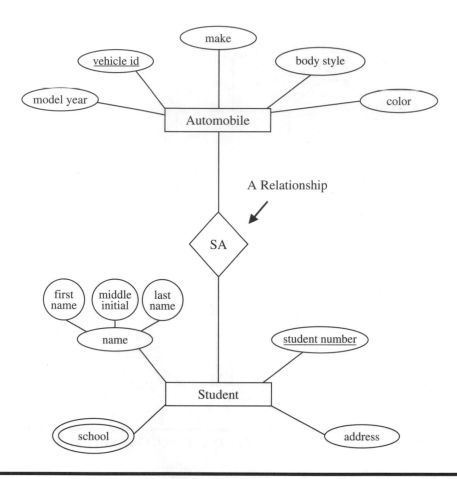

Figure 3.6 An ER Diagram of the STUDENT–AUTOMOBILE Database with an "Unknown," "Yet-To-Be-Determined" Relationship

Checkpoint 3.1

1. Can the nature of an entity change over time? Explain.
2. What is a relationship?
3. What are the differences between an entity and a relationship?
4. When would it be preferable to consider an attribute an entity? Why or why not?
5. Does it make sense to have an entity with one attribute?

Does a Relationship Exist?

Some situations may unfold where a relationship might be unclear. For example, consider this user description of a desired database:

> Create a database for CUSTOMERS and SUPPLIERS. CUSTOMERS will have a name, address, phone number, and customer number. SUPPLIERS will have a supplier number, name, and address.

In this database, we clearly have two entities — CUSTOMER and SUPPLIER. We want to store information about customers (their name, address, etc.) and suppliers (supplier number, name, etc.). But what is the connection between the two?

What we have here is an incomplete, vague user description from which to design our database. The connection for the company that wants the database is that it has both customers and suppliers; however, what the company may not realize is that the relationship from CUSTOMER to SUPPLIER is via a COMPANY or a VENDOR, and not a direct relationship. So, what we have so far in this description is two different parts of a company database, one for customers and one for suppliers. If we later have some other entity such as "inventory" or "vendor" that is related to customers and to suppliers, there may be linking entities and relationships. For now with just two unrelated ideas — customer and supplier — there is no apparent relationship, so the thing to do would be to leave any relationship off of the overall diagram until more information is elicited from the user. It may even be that two unrelated databases need to be developed.

Attribute or Relationship?

Sometimes it may be unclear as to whether something is an attribute or a relationship. Both attributes and relationships express something about an entity. An entity's attributes express qualities in terms of properties or characteristics. Relationships express associations with other entities.

Suppose we are constructing a library database. Suppose further that we create another primary entity BOOK that has an attribute, borrower. In some cases, an attribute construct is likely to be inappropriate for expressing an optional association that really ought to be a relationship between two entities. As a side issue, borrower would require the use of a null value for those BOOK entities that were not loaned out. In reality, only a very small fraction of a library's books are on loan at any given time. Thus, the "borrower" attribute would be null for most of the BOOK entities. This recurrence of many nulls might indicate that the attribute borrower_name could be an entity. If a BORROWER entity were created, and the association between the entities BOOK and BORROWER was explicitly stated as a relationship, the database designer would likely be closer to putting attributes and entities in their correct places. It is important to understand the distinction between the types of information that can be expressed as attributes and those that should be treated as relationships and entities.

Checkpoint 3.2

1. Are relationships between two entities permanent, or can the nature of this relationship change over time?
2. Are attributes of an entity permanent?
3. Does there always exist a relationship between two entities?
4. What is a binary relationship?

Our ER elicitation and design methodology is now this:

ER Design Methodology

Step 1: Select one, primary entity from the database requirements description and show attributes to be recorded for that entity. Label keys if appropriate and show some sample data.

Step 2: Use structured English for entities, attributes, and keys to describe the database that has been elicited.

Step 3: Examine attributes in the primary entity (possibly with user assistance) to find out if information about one of the attributes is to be recorded.

Step 3a: If information about an attribute is needed, make the attribute an entity, and then

Step 3b: Define the relationship back to the original entity.

Step 4: If another entity is appropriate, draw the second entity with its attributes. Repeat step 2 to see if this entity should be further split into more entities.

Step 5: Connect entities with relationships if relationships exist.

Step 6: Show some sample data.

Chapter Summary

Entities, attributes, and relationships were defined in Chapter 2. However, in real life, while trying to design databases, it is often difficult to determine whether something should be an attribute, entity, or a relationship. This chapter discussed ways (techniques) to determine whether something should be an entity, attribute, or a relationship.

This chapter also introduced the concept of binary relationships. Real-life databases will have more than one entity, so this chapter developed the ER diagram from a one-entity diagram to a two-entity diagram, and showed how to determine and depict binary relationships between the two entities using the Chen-like model. Because the concept of relationships was only introduced, and structural constraints of relationships have not yet been discussed, we have not included mapping rules in this chapter.

Chapter 3 Exercises

Exercise 3.1

Draw an ER diagram (using the Chen-like model) for an entity called HOTEL and include no fewer than five attributes for the entity. Of the five attributes, include at least one composite attribute and one multi-valued attribute.

Exercise 3.2

Let us suppose that we reconsider our STUDENT example and the only attributes of STUDENT are student number and name. Let us suppose that we have another entity called HIGH SCHOOL, which is going to be the high school from which the student graduated. For the HIGH SCHOOL entity, we will record the high school name and the location (meaning, city and state). Draw the ER diagram using the concise form (as Figure 2.1, bottom). What would you name the relationship here? Write out the grammar for the relationship between the two entities.

Exercise 3.3

Suppose that a college had one dormitory with many rooms. The DORMITORY entity, which is actually a "dormitory room" entity because there is only one dorm, has the attributes room number and single/double (meaning that there are private rooms and double rooms). Let us suppose that the STUDENT entity in this case contains the attributes student number, student name, and home telephone number. Draw the ER diagram in the Chen-like model linking up the two entities. Name your relationships. Write out the grammar for the relationship between the two entities.

Exercise 3.4

We have two entities, a PLANE and a PILOT, and describe the relationship between the two entities as "A PILOT *flies* a PLANE." What should the relationship read from the other entity's side?

Exercise 3.5

Complete the methodology by adding sample data to Figures 3.3, 3.5, as well as to Exercises 1, 2, 3, and 4.

References

Atzeni, P., Ceri, S., Paraboschi, S., and Torlone, R., *Database Systems,* McGraw-Hill, New York, 1999.

Elmasri, R. and Navathe, S.B., *Fundamentals of Database Systems*, 3rd ed., Addison-Wesley, Reading, MA, 2000.

Lochovsky, F.H., Ed., *Entity-Relationship Approach to Database Design and Querying,* Elsevier Science, New York, 1990.

Case Study: West Florida Mall (continued)

In Chapter 2 we chose our primary entity, MALL, and used structured English to describe it, its attributes and keys, and then we mapped MALL to a relational database (with some sample data). In this chapter we continue to develop this case study by looking at steps 3, 4, and 5, of the ER design methodology, and then mapping the entities that are developed into a relational database with some sample data.

Step 3 says:

Step 3: Examine attributes in the primary entity (with user assistance) to find out if information about one of the entities is to be recorded.

Upon reexamining the attributes of the primary entity, MALL, it appears that we need to store information about the attribute, store. So we look at Step 3a, which says:

Step 3a: If information about an attribute is needed, then make the attribute an entity, and then Step 3b.

So, turning the attribute, store, into an entity we have (repeating step 2):

The Entity

> This database records data about a STORE. For each STORE in the database, we record a store name (sname), a store number (snum), a store location (sloc), and departments (dept).

The Attributes for STORE

> For each STORE, there will always be one and only one sname (store name). The value for sname will not be subdivided.

> For each STORE, there will always be one and only one snum (store number). The value for snum will be unique, and not be subdivided.

> For each STORE, we will record a sloc (store location). There will be one sloc recorded for each STORE. The value for sloc will not be subdivided.

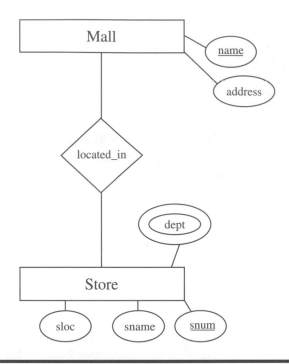

Figure 3.7   An ER Diagram of the Mall Database Thus Far

For each STORE, we will record depts (departments). There will be more than one depts recorded for each STORE. The value for depts will not be subdivided.

The Keys

For each STORE, we will assume that the snum will be unique.

Note: Once STORE is made into an entity, the attribute, store, is removed from the entity MALL, as shown in Figure 3.7.

Having defined STORE, we now need to follow Step 3b, which says:

Step 3b: Define the relationship back to the original entity.

There is a relationship, located_in, between STORE and MALL. This is shown in Figure 3.7.

Next, Step 4 says:

Step 4: If another entity is appropriate, draw the second entity with its attributes. Repeat Step 2 to see if this entity should be further split into more entities.

We will select another entity, STORE_MANAGER. Now, repeating step 2 for STORE_MANAGER:

The Entity

This database records data about a STORE_MANAGER.

For each STORE_MANAGER in the database, we record a store manager name (sm_name), store manager social security number (sm_ssn), and store manager salary (sm_salary).

The Attributes for STORE_MANAGER

For each STORE_MANAGER, there will always be one and only one sm_name (store manager name). The value for sm_name will not be subdivided.

For each STORE_MANAGER, there will always be one and only one sm_ssn (store manager ssn). The value for sm_ssn will be unique, and not be subdivided.

For each STORE_MANAGER, we will record a sm_salary (store manager salary). There will be one and only one sm_salary recorded for each STORE_MANAGER. The value for sm_salary will not be subdivided.

The Keys

For each STORE_MANAGER, we will assume that the sm_ssn will be unique.

Having defined STORE_MANAGER, we now follow Step 5, which says:

Step 5: Connect entities with relationships if relationships exist.

There is a relationship, manages, between STORE and STORE_MANAGER. This is shown in Figure 3.8.

Then we select our next primary entity, STORE_OWNER. Now, repeating step 2 for STORE_OWNER:

The Entity

This database records data about a STORE_OWNER. For each STORE_OWNER in the database, we record a store owner name (so_name), store owner social security number (so_ssn), store owner's office phone (so_off_phone), and store owner address (so_address).

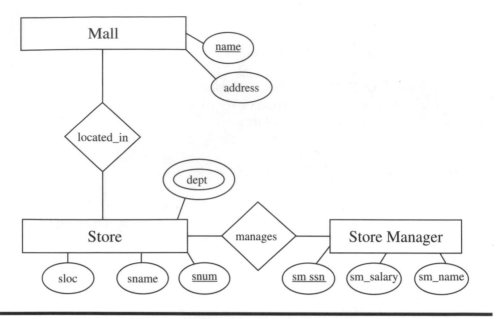

Figure 3.8   An ER Diagram of West Florida Mall Database Developing

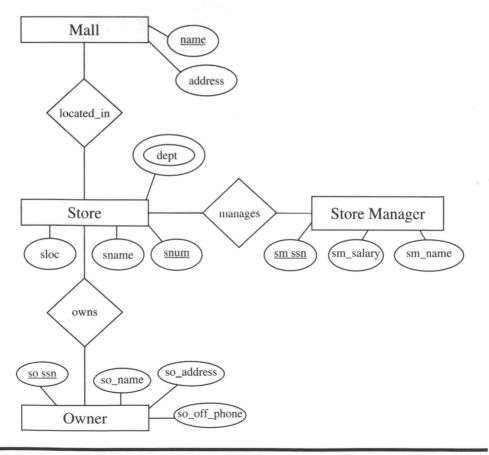

Figure 3.9   An ER Diagram of West Florida Mall with Four Entities

The Attributes for STORE_OWNER

For each STORE_OWNER, there will always be one and only one so_name (store owner name). The value for so_name will not be subdivided.

For each STORE_OWNER, there will always be one and only one so_ssn (store owner ssn). The value for so_ssn will be unique, and will not be subdivided.

For each STORE_OWNER, there will always be one and only one so_off_phone (store owner office phone). The value for so_off_phone will be unique, and will not be subdivided.

For each STORE_OWNER, we will record a so_address (store owner address). There will be one and only one so_address recorded for each STORE_OWNER. The value for so_address will not be subdivided.

The Keys

For each STORE_OWNER, we will assume that the so_ssn will be unique. Having defined STORE_OWNER, we now follow Step 5, which says:

Step 5: Connect entities with relationships if relationships exist.

There is a relationship, owns, between STORE and OWNER. This is shown in Figure 3.9.

Mapping the Entity to a Relational Database

Having described the entities, attributes, and keys, the next step would be to map the entities to a relational database. We will also show some data for the entities developed, in this part of the case study (the mappings of the relationships will be shown at the end of Chapter 4).

Relations for the MALL Entity:

The first two relations, MALL–Store and MALL are the same as they were in Chapter 2:

MALL–Store	
name	store_name
West Florida Mall	Penney's
West Florida Mall	Sears
West Florida Mall	Dollar Store
West Florida Mall	Rex
Cordova Mall	Dillards
:	
:	

MALL	
name	*address*
West Florida Mall	N Davis Hwy, Pensacola, FL
Cordova Mall	9th Avenue, Pensacola, FL
Navy Mall	Navy Blvd, Pensacola, FL
BelAir Mall	10th Avenue, Mobile, AL

Relations for the STORE Entity:

The entity, STORE, has a multi-valued attribute, depts, so we will again have to use mapping rule M1 and M1c (as stated in Chapter 2) to map this entity. First, we will show the relation with the multi-valued attribute excised, and then we will show the relation with the multi-valued attribute. (Note: We are developing this database for the West Florida Mall, so we will map only its stores.)

Relation with the Multi-Valued Attribute Excised:

STORE		
sloc	*sname*	*snum*
Rm 101	Penney's	1
Rm 102	Sears	2
Rm 109	Dollar Store	3
Rm 110	Rex	4

Relation with the Multi-Valued Attribute:

STORE–dept	
snum	*depts*
1	Tall men's clothing
1	Women's clothing
1	Children's clothing
1	Men's clothing
.	
2	Men's clothing
2	Women's clothing
2	Children's clothing
2	Hardware
.	
.	.
.	

Relation for the STORE MANAGER Entity (using mapping rule M1 and M1a):

	STORE MANAGER	
sm_ssn	*sm_name*	*sm_salary*
234–987–0988	Saha	45,900
456–098–0987	Becker	43,989
928–982–9882	Ford	44,000
283–972–0927	Raja	38,988

Relation for the OWNER Entity (using mapping rule M1 and M1a):

		OWNER	
so_ssn	*so_name*	*so_off_phone*	*so_address*
879–987–0987	Earp	(850)474–2093	1195 Gulf Breeze Pkwy, Pensacola, FL
826–098–0877	Sardar	(850)474–9873	109 Navy Blvd, Pensacola, FL
928–088–7654	Bagui	(850)474–9382	89 Highland Heights, Tampa, FL
982–876–8766	Bush	(850)474–9283	987 Middle Tree, Mobile, AL

So far our relational database has developed into (without the data):
[Note: The primary keys are underlined.]

MALL-Store

name	store_name

MALL

name	address

STORE

sloc	sname	snum

STORE-dept

snum	depts

OWNER

so_ssn	so_name	so_off_phone	so_address

STORE MANAGER

sm_ssn	sm_name	sm_salary

This case study will be continued at the end of Chapter 4.

Chapter 4

Extending Relationships/ Structural Constraints

Chapter Topics

In Chapters 2 and 3, we introduced some components of ER diagrams, including entities, attributes, and relationships. It is really insufficient for requirements elicitation to define relationships without also defining what are called *structural constraints*. Structural constraints are information about how two (or more) entities are related to one another. There are two types of structural constraints: cardinality and participation.

In this chapter, in addition to the structural constraints of relationships, we want to introduce a grammar to describe what we have drawn. The grammar will help with the requirements elicitation process, as we will specify a template for the English that can be imposed on a diagram, which will in turn make us say exactly what the diagram means. This chapter develops steps 6 and 7 of the ER design methodology. Step 6 states the nature of a relationship in English, and step 7 discusses presenting the database (designed so far) to the user.

Mapping rules for relationships are also developed and discussed with examples and sample data. At the end of the chapter, we also continue the running case study that we began in Chapter 2 and continued in Chapter 3.

The Cardinality Ratio of a Relationship

Cardinality is a rough measure of the number of entities (one or more) that will be related to another entity (or entities). For example, there are four ways in which the entities AUTOMOBILE and STUDENT can be "numerically involved" in a relationship: one-to-one (1:1), many-to-one (M:1), one-to-many (1:M), and many-to-many (M:N).

One-to-One (1:1)

In this type of relationship, one entity is associated with one other entity, and vice versa. Take, for example, if in our drive relationship (shown in Figure 4.1), we stated that one automobile is driven by one student and one student drives one automobile, then the student/automobile relationship would be one-to-one, symbolically:

$$\text{STUDENT:AUTOMOBILE} \ :: \ 1:1$$

Diagramatically we can represent a 1:1 relationship as shown in Figure 4A (Batani, Ceri, and Navathe, 1992).

Many-to-One (M:1)

If the SA (STUDENT:AUTOMOBILE) relationship (shown in Figure 3.6) were many-to-one, we would say that many students are associated with one automobile and one automobile is associated with many students; that is:

$$\text{STUDENT:AUTOMOBILE::M:1}$$

We have intentionally used the verb phrase "is associated with" in place of drive because the statement "many students drive one automobile" can be taken in a variety of ways. Also, using a specific verb for a relationship is not always best when the diagram is first drawn, unless the analyst is absolutely sure that the verb correctly describes the user's intention. We could have also used the verb phrase "is related to" instead of "is associated with" if we wanted to be uncommitted about the exact verb to use.

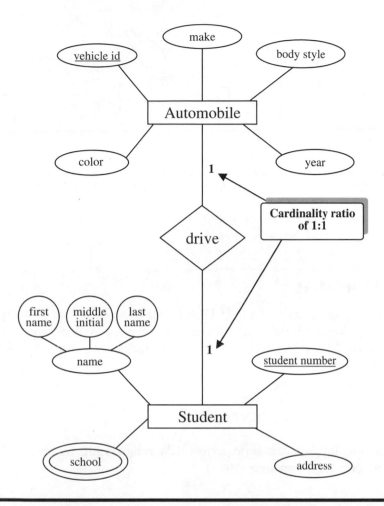

Figure 4.1   An ER Diagram of the STUDENT-AUTOMOBILE Database with the Relationship Name, *drive,* and Showing the Cardinality Ratios

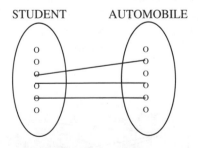

Figure 4A   One-to-One Relationship STUDENT:AUTOMOBILE::1:1

We will tighten the language used to describe relationships presently, but what does an STUDENT:AUTOMOBILE::M:1 relationship imply? It would represent a situation where perhaps a family owned one car and that car was driven by multiple people in the family.

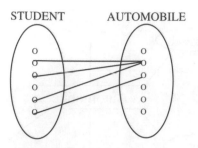

Figure 4B   Many-to-One Relationship STUDENT:AUTOMOBILE::M:1

Diagramatically, we can represent a M:1 relationship as shown in Figure 4B (Batani, Ceri, and Navathe, 1992).

One-to-Many (1:M)

The sense of a one-to-many SA (STUDENT:AUTOMOBILE) relationship (shown in Figure 3.6) would be that a student is associated with many automobiles and an automobile is associated with one student. Clearly, if we define a relationship as 1:M (or M:1), then we need to be very clear about which entity is 1 and which is M. Here:

STUDENT:AUTOMOBILE::1:M

Diagramatically, we can represent a 1:M relationship as shown in Figure 4C (Batani, Ceri, and Navathe, 1992).

Many-to-Many (M:N)

In many-to-many relationships, many occurrences of one entity are associated with many of the other. Many-to-many is depicted as M:N, as in M of one thing related to N of another thing. Older database texts called this an M:M relationship, but newer books use M:N to indicate that the number of things related is not presumed to be equal (the values of M and N are likely to be different).

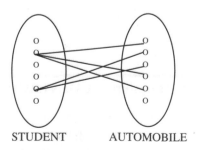

Figure 4C   One-to-Many Relationship STUDENT:AUTOMOBILE::1:M

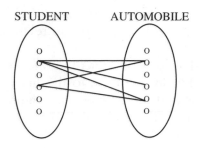

Figure 4D   Many-to-Many Relationship STUDENT:AUTOMOBILE::M:N

If our SA relationship were many-to-many, a student would be associated with many automobiles and an automobile with many students:

STUDENT:AUTOMOBILE::M:N

In this case (if we assumed SA = drive, as shown in Figure 3.6), multiple students can drive multiple cars (hopefully not all at the same time) and multiple cars can be driven by multiple students. Picture, for example, a family that has multiple cars and any one family member can drive any of the cars and any car can be driven by any family member.

Diagramatically, we can represent an M:N relationship as shown in Figure 4D (Batani, Ceri, and Navathe, 1992).

In expressing cardinality, this x:x ratio, where x = 1 or M(N), is called a cardinality ratio.

Which way do we depict the actual situation for our students and automobiles? This is a very interesting question. The answer is that we are to model reality as defined by our user. We listen to the user, make some assumptions, and draw the model. We then pass our model back to the user using a structured English that the user then approves or corrects.

A trap in ER design is to try to model every situation for every possibility. This cannot be done. The point of creating a database is normally a local situation that will be governed by the systems analysis (software engineering) process. In classical systems analysis, the analyst hears a user, creates a specification, and then presents the result back to the user. Here, the analyst (the database analyst/designer) models the reality that the user experiences — not what every database in the world should look like. If the user disagrees, then the analyst can easily modify the conceptual model, but there has to be a meeting of the minds on what the model is to depict.

In our STUDENT:AUTOMOBILE example, the choice we will make will be that one student is associated with (drives) one automobile. While clearly one can think of exceptions to this case, we are going to adopt a model, and the sense of the model is that we have to choose how we will identify the relationship between the entities as well as the information that we intend to put in the entities themselves. Bear in mind that we are dealing with a conceptual model that could change, depending on the reality of the situation; however, we have to choose some sort of model to begin with, and the one we are choosing is a one-to-one relationship between students and automobiles.

In the Chen-like model, we will depict the one-to-oneness of this relationship by adding the cardinality numbers to the lines on the ER diagram that connect the relationships and the entities (see Figure 4.1).

In Figure 4.1 we put a "1" on the line between the entity box for the STUDENT and the diamond box for the relationship, and we put another "1" on the line between the diamond relationship and the entity box for the AUTOMOBILE. These 1's loosely mean that a student is related to one automobile and an automobile is related to one student. We must be quite careful in saying exactly what this relationship means. It does not mean that one student owns one automobile or a student pays insurance for an automobile. In our model, we mean that a student will drive, at most, one automobile on a college campus. Further, we are saying that an automobile will be driven by one and only one student. Because we are clarifying (refining) the database, we try to settle on the name of the relationship to include the concept that we are modeling — driving — by naming the relationship drive. Again, see Figure 4.1 for the renamed model with 1:1 cardinality.

Participation: Full/Partial

It is likely that on any campus, not all students will drive an automobile. For our model, we could assume that normally all of the automobiles on the campus are associated with a student. (We are for the moment excluding faculty and staff driving, and modeling the student/automobile relationship.)

To show that every automobile is driven by a student, but not every student drives an automobile, we will enhance our Chen-like model of ER diagrams by putting a double line between the relationship diamond and the AUTOMOBILE entity to indicate that every automobile is driven by one student. Put another way, every automobile in the database participates in the relationship. From the student side, we leave the line between the STUDENT entity and the relationship as a single line to indicate that not every student drives an automobile. Some students will not participate in the drive relationship because they do not drive a car on campus. The single/double lines are called participation constraints (a.k.a., optionality constraints) and are depicted in Figure 4.2.

The double line indicates full participation. Some designers prefer to call this participation mandatory. The point is that if part of a relationship is mandatory or full, you cannot have a null value (a missing value) for that attribute in relationships. In our case, if an automobile is in the database, it must be related to some student.

The single line, partial participation, is also called optional. The sense of partial, optional participation is that there could be students who do not have a relationship to an automobile.

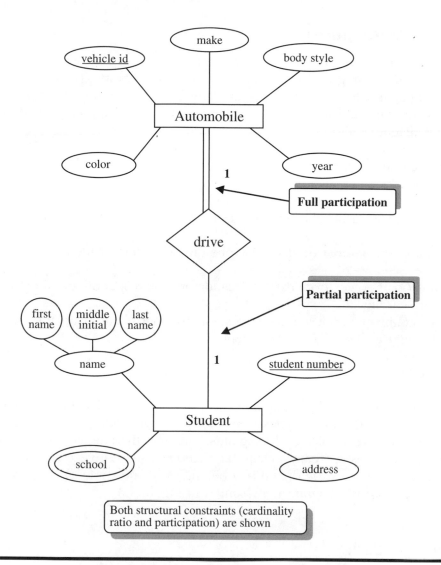

Figure 4.2 An ER Diagram of the STUDENT–AUTOMOBILE Database with the Relationship Name, *drive*

Checkpoint 4.1

1. What are structural constraints?
2. What kind of information does the cardinality ratio give us?
3. In how many different ways can two entities be involved in a cardinality relationship? Give examples.
4. What kind of information does the participation constraint give us?
5. Is it always necessary to have cardinality ratios as well as participation constraints in the same ER diagram? Why? Explain.

English Descriptions

We would now like to tighten the grammar that describes how a relationship affects entities using our structural constraints, and to adopt a standard way of stating the relationship. The standard language should appear on the model, or at least with it. Further, using a standard language approach to describe the ER diagrams allows us to not only close the loop with the user in the systems analysis process, but also facilitates feedback and "nails down" the exact meaning of the relationship.

In the Chen-like model, the double lines define full participation, as in "automobiles fully participate in the drive relationship." Better yet, the double lines invite us to state the relationship as:

> Automobiles **must** be driven by one (and only one) student.

The *must* part comes from the full (mandatory) participation and the *one* part from the cardinality.

The grammar for describing partial or optional relationship for the STUDENT entity to the AUTOMOBILE entity would be:

> Students **may** drive one and only one automobile.

The *may* comes from the single line leaving the STUDENT entity box and the "one and only one" part comes from the cardinality. The point is that when expressing the sense of the ER diagrams, one uses the language that conveys what the relationship really means (i.e., students may drive one automobile and automobiles must be driven by one and only one student). A graphic on how to read an ER diagram is presented in Figure 4.3.

Tighter English

We strongly recommend that an English sentence accompany each diagram to reinforce the meaning of the figure. Refer to Figure 4.3. English is often an ambiguous language. The statement that:

> Automobiles must be driven by one and only one student.

actually means that:

> Automobiles, which are in the database, must be driven by one and only one student.

It does not mean that:

> One particular student drives some automobiles.

Another way to put this is:

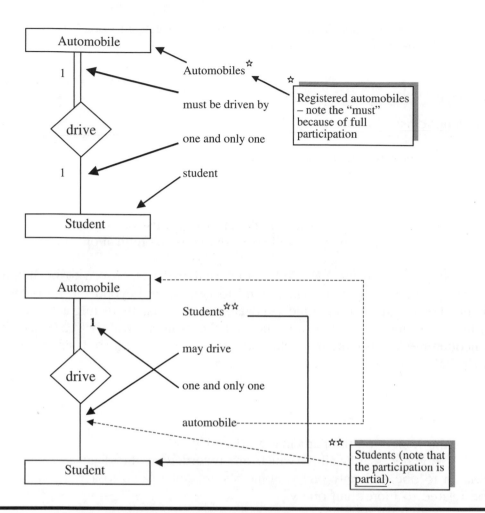

Figure 4.3 An ER Diagram of the STUDENT–AUTOMOBILE Database. Translating the Diagram into English

> Automobiles must be driven by one and only one student driver. Students may drive one and only one automobile.

To relieve ambiguity in the statement of the relationship, we will take the English statement from the relationship we have illustrated, and define four pattern possibilities for expressing our relationship. All binary relationships must be stated in two ways from both sides. As you will see, we will try to stick to the exact pattern match in the following examples, but common sense and reasonable grammar should prevail in cases where the pattern does not quite fit. There is nothing wrong with restating the precise language to make it more clear, but you have to say the same thing!

Pattern 1 — x:y::k:1

From the k side, full participation (k = 1 or M):

x's, which are recorded in the database, must be related to one and only one y. No x is related to more than one y.

Example:

Student:Advisor::M:1

> Students **must** be advised by one advisor.

or

> Students, which are recorded in the database, **must** be advised by one and only one advisor. No student is advised by more than one advisor.

The phrase "which are recorded in the database" has proven to be helpful because some database designers tend to generalize beyond the problem at hand. For example, one could reasonably argue that there might be a case where thus-and-so are true/not true, but the point is, will that case ever be encountered in this particular database? The negative statement is often helpful to solidify the meaning of the relationship.

Pattern 2 — x:y::k:1

From the k side, partial participation (k = 1 or M):
x, but not necessarily all x (which are recorded in the database), may be related to one and only one y. Some x's are not related to a y. x's may not be related to more than one y.

Example:

Student:Fraternity::M:1

> Some students join a fraternity.

which becomes:

> Students, but not necessarily all students (which are recorded in the database), **may** join a fraternity. Some students **may** not join a fraternity. Students may not join more than one fraternity.

Pattern 3 — x:y::k:M

From the k side, full participation (k = 1 or M):
x's, which are recorded in the database, must be related to many (one or more) y's. Sometimes it is helpful to include a phrase such as: No x is related

to a non y (or) Non x are not related to a y. The negative will depend on the sense of the statement.

Example:

Automobile:Student::M:N

> Automobiles are driven by (registered to) many students

which means:

> Automobiles, which are recorded in our database, **must** be driven by many (one or more) students.

There are several ideas implied here. First, we are only talking about vehicles which are registered at this school. Second, in this database, only student cars are registered. Third, if an automobile from this database is driven, it has to be registered and driven by a student. Fourth, the "one or more" comes from the cardinality constraint. Fifth, there is a strong temptation to say something about the y, the M side back to the x, but this should be avoided as this is covered elsewhere in another pattern, and because we discourage inferring other relationships from the one covered. For example, one might try to say here that all students drive cars or all students are related to a vehicle — neither statement is true.

Pattern 4 — x:y::k:M

From the k side, partial participation (k = 1 or M):
x, but not necessarily all x, (which are recorded in the database) may be related to many (zero or more) y's. Some x may not be related to a y.

Example:

Course:Book::k:M

> Some courses may require (use) many books.

which, restated, becomes:

> Courses, but not necessarily all courses, (which are recorded in the database) **may** use many (zero or more) textbooks. Some courses **may** not require textbooks.

Note that due to partial participation (the single lines), the phrase "zero or more," is used for cardinality. If a relationship is modeled with the patterns we have used and then the English sounds incorrect, it may be that the wrong model has been chosen. Generally, the grammatical expression will be most useful in (1) restating the designed database to a naïve user, and (2) checking the meaning on the designed database among the designers. The complete version of the English may eventually prove tiresome to a database designer, but one should never lose track of the fact that a statement like "x are related to one y" can be interpreted in several ways unless it is "nailed down" with constraints stated in an unambiguous way. Furthermore, a negation statement may be useful to elicit a requirements definition, although at times the negation is so cumbersome it may be left off entirely. What we are saying is to add the negative or other noncontradictory grammar if it makes sense and helps with requirements elicitation. The danger in adding sentences is that we may end up with contradictory or confusing remarks.

Summary of the above Patterns and Relationships

Pattern 1:

Relationship is   **x:y::1(full):1**
Diagramatically shown by Figure 4E

Pattern 1:

Relationship is   **x:y::M(full):1**
Diagramatically shown by Figure 4F
    This is a very common form of a relationship which implies that an instance of ENTITY1 can only exist for one (and only one) of ENTITY2.

Pattern 2:

Relationship is   **x:y::1(partial):1**
Diagramatically shown by Figure 4G

Pattern 2:

Relationship is   **x:y::M(partial):1**
Diagramatically shown by Figure 4H
    In this case, some instances in ENTITY1 and ENTITY2 can exist without the relationship to the other entity.

Pattern 3:

Relationship is   **x:y::1(full):M**
Diagramatically shown by Figure 4I

Pattern 3:

Relationship is   **x:y::M(full):N**
Diagramatically shown by Figure 4J

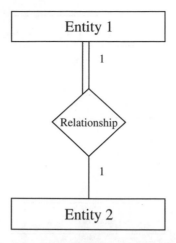

Figure 4E   Chen Model of 1(full):1 Relationship — Pattern 1

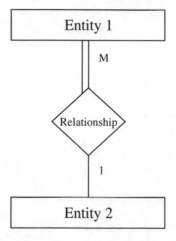

Figure 4F   Chen Model of M(full):1 Relationship — Pattern 1

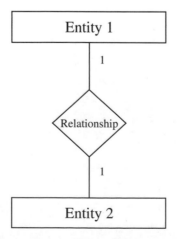

Figure 4G   Chen Model of 1(partial):1 Relationship — Pattern 2

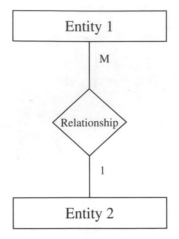

Figure 4H   Chen Model of M(partial):1 Relationship — Pattern 2

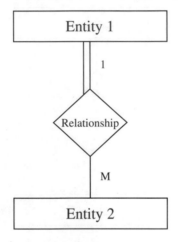

Figure 4I   Chen Model of 1(full):M Relationship — Pattern 3

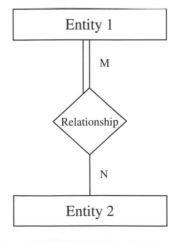

Figure 4J   Chen Model of M(full):N Relationship — Pattern 3

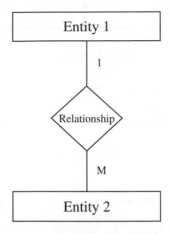

Figure 4K   Chen Model of 1(partial):M Relationship — Pattern 4

Pattern 4:

Relationship is   **x:y::1(partial):M**
Diagramatically shown by Figure 4K

Pattern 4:

Relationship is   **x:y::M(partial):N**
Diagramatically shown by Figure 4L

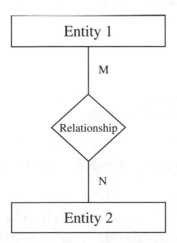

Figure 4L   Chen Model of M(partial):N Relationship — Pattern 4

Checkpoint 4.2

1. Sketch an ER diagram that shows the participation ratios (full/partial) and cardinalities for the following:
   a. Students must be advised by one advisor.
   b. Students, but not necessarily all students, may join a fraternity. Some students may not join a fraternity. Students may not join more than one fraternity.

Our refined methodology may now be restated with the relationship information added:

ER Design Methodology

Step 1: Select one, primary entity from the database requirements description and show attributes to be recorded for that entity. Label keys, if appropriate, and show some sample data.

Step 2: Use structured English for entities, attributes, and keys to describe the database that has been elicited.

Step 3: Examine attributes in the primary entity (possibly with user assistance) to find out if information about one of the attributes is to be recorded.

Step 3a: If information about an attribute is needed, then make the attribute an entity, and then

Step 3b: Define the relationship back to the original entity.

Step 4: If another entity is appropriate, draw the second entity with its attributes. Repeat step 2 to see if this entity should be further split into more entities.

Step 5: Connect entities with relationships if relationships exist.

Step 6: State the exact nature of the relationships in structured English from all sides. For example, if a relationship is A:B::1:M, then there is a relationship from A(1) to B(M) and from B(M) back to A(1).

Step 7: Present the "as designed" database to the user, complete with the English for entities, attributes, keys, and relationships. Refine the diagram as necessary.

Step 8: Show some sample data.

Some Examples of Other Relationships

In this section, we consider three other examples of relationships — the two 1:M relationships and an M:N relationship — in more detail in order to practice and further clarify the process we have presented.

An Example of the One-to-Many Relationship (1:M)

Relationships that are 1:M or M:1 are really relative views of the same problem. When specifying 1:M or M:1, we need to be especially careful to specify which entity is 1 (one) and which is M. The designation is really which view is more natural for the database designer. As an example of a 1:M relationship, consider dorm rooms and students. One dorm room may have many students living in it, and many students can live in one dorm room. So, the relationship between dorm room and students would be considered a one-to-many (1:M:: DORM:STUDENT) situation and would be depicted as in Figure 4.4 (without attributes). We let the term DORM mean dorm room.

In Figure 4.4 (the Chen-like model), the name that we chose for the DORM–STUDENT relationship was occupy.

Note that not all dorms have students living in them, and hence the participation of dorms in the relationship is partial. Informally,

Dorms may be occupied by many students.

Furthermore, all students may not live in dorms: therefore, the relationship of STUDENT to DORM is also partial:

Students may occupy a dorm room.

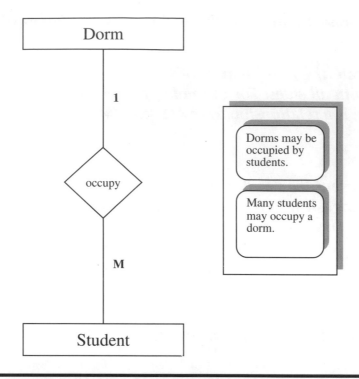

Figure 4.4   An ER Diagram (without Attributes) of a 1:M Relationship

Now let us restate the relationships in the short and long English forms. For the first statement: "Dorms may be occupied by many students" — this fits Pattern 4 — x:y::1(partial):M.

Pattern 4 — 1:M, from 1 side partial participation

"Some x are related to many y."

Therefore, the more precise statement is:

x, but not necessarily all x, (which are recorded in the database) may be related to many (zero or more) y's. Some x are not related to a y ...

or

Dorms, but not necessarily all dorms, (which are recorded in the database) **may** be occupied by many (zero or more) students.

For the inverse relationship: Students may occupy a dorm room — this fits Pattern 2 — M(partial):1.

Pattern 2 — M(partial):1, from M side, optional participation

"Some x are related to one y."

Therefore, the long "translation" of the statement is:

> x, but not necessarily all x, (which are recorded in the database) may be related to one and only one y. Some x may not be related to y. [No x is related to more than one y.] [...] indicates optional clarification.

This x and y notation resolves into, x = students, y = dorms, and hence:

> Students, but not necessarily all students, (which are recorded in the database) **may** occupy one and only one dorm. Many students **may** not occupy one dorm room. No student occupies more than one dorm.

An Example of the Many-to-One Relationship (M:1)

Let us assume for a database that a school or college that we are modeling has student parking lots. And let us further assume that every student is assigned to park his or her car in some specific parking area. We then have an entity called PARKING AREA, which will have parking locations that will be described by some descriptive notation such as East Area #7, North Area #28, etc. In this case, if we viewed many automobiles as assigned to the one parking area and parking area as containing many automobiles, we could depict this relationship as a many-to-one, M:1::AUTOMOBILE:PARKING AREA. This diagram is shown in Figure 4.5 (again, without attributes).

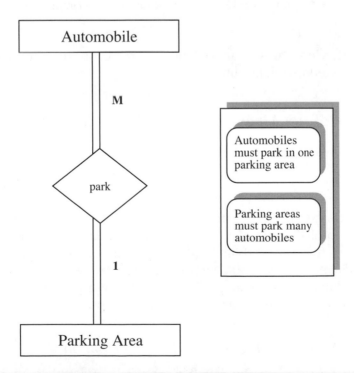

Figure 4.5   An ER Diagram (without Attributes) of a M:1 Relationship

We have depicted the relationship participation between automobile and parking area as full in both instances — meaning that all automobiles have one parking area and all parking areas are assigned to student's automobiles.

The grammatical expressions of this relationship are:

Pattern 1 — M:1, from the M side, full participation

x, which are recorded in the database, must be related to one and only one y. No x are related to more than one y.

   x = automobile, y = parking area, relationship = park

> Automobiles, which are recorded in the database, must be parked in one and only one parking area. No automobiles may be parked in more than one parking area.

And the inverse:

Pattern 3 — 1:M, from the 1 side, full participation

x, which are recorded in the database, must be related to many (one or more) y's. [No x is related to a non y (or) Non x are not related to a y. (The negative will depend on the sense of the statement.)]

> Parking areas, which are recorded in the database, must park many (one or more) automobiles. No parking areas contain non-student automobiles.

This means that no parking areas that we are recording data about in this database parks non-student automobiles.

An Example of the Many-to-Many Relationship (M:N)

The classic example that we will study here is students taking courses. At the outset we know that students take (enroll in) many courses and that any course is populated by many students. The basic diagram for the student-course relationship is that as shown in Figure 4.6.

We have chosen the word enroll to depict the relationship. The participation of students in enroll is depicted as full (mandatory); course enrollment is depicted as partial. This choice was arbitrary, as both could be full or partial, depending on user needs and desires. Look carefully at the exact grammatical expressions and note the impact of choosing full in one case and partial in the other.

The grammatical expressions of this relationship are:

Pattern 3 — M:N, from the M side, full participation

x, which are recorded in the database, must be related to many (one or more) y. [No x is related to a non y (or) Non x are not related to a y (or)

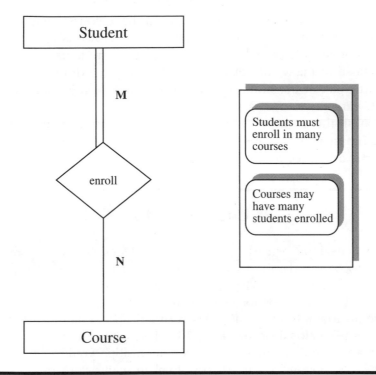

Figure 4.6   An ER Diagram (without Attributes) of a M:N Relationship

No x is not related to a y. (The negative will depend on the sense of the statement.)]

x = students, y = courses, relationship = enroll

Students, which are recorded in the database, **must** be enrolled in many (one or more) courses.

And for the inverse:

Pattern 4 — M:N, from the M side, partial participation

x, but not necessarily all x, (which are recorded in the database) may be related to many (one or more) y. Some x may not be related to y.

x = course, y = student, relationship = enroll

Courses, but not necessarily all courses, (which are recorded in the database) may enroll many (one or more) students. Some courses may not enroll students.

This "course partiality" likely reflects courses that are in the database, but are not currently enrolling students. It could mean potential courses, or courses that are no longer offered. Of course, if the course is in the database only if students are enrolled, then the participation constraint becomes full and the sense of the entity relationship changes.

Also, this database tells us that while we can have courses without students, we only store information about active students. Obviously we could make the student connection partial and hence store all students — even inactive ones. We chose to make the relationships the way we did to make the point that the participation constraint is to depict reality — the reality of what the user might want to store data about.

Note that all the examples in this chapter deal with only two entities; that is, they are binary relationships. The example in the following section provides yet another example of a binary relationship.

Checkpoint 4.3

1. Give an example of a 1(full):1 relationship? Does such a relationship always have to be mandatory? Explain with examples.
2. Give an example of a 1(partial):1 relationship? Does such a relationship always have to be optional? Explain with examples.
3. Give an example of an M(full):N relationship? Would such a relationship always be optional or mandatory? Explain with examples.
4. Give an example of an M(partial):N relationship? Would such a relationship always be optional or mandatory? Explain with examples.

One Final Example

As a final example to conclude the chapter, we present one more problem and the methodology.[1] Consider a model for a simplified airport that records PASSENGERS and FLIGHTS. Suppose that the attributes of PASSENGER are name, articles of luggage, and frequent flyer number. Suppose the attributes for FLIGHT are flight number, destination, time of departure, and estimated time of arrival. Draw the ER diagram.

Note: We are leaving out many things (attributes) that we could consider about our airport; but for the sake of an example, assume that this is all the information that we choose to record.

Here is the solution:

ER Design Methodology

Step 1: Select one, primary entity from the database requirements description and show attributes to be recorded for that entity. Label keys if appropriate and show some sample data.

---

[1] Modeled after Elmasri and Navathe (2000).

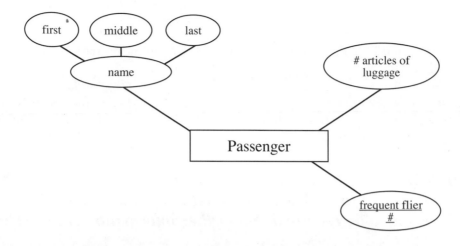

Figure 4.7   The PASSENGER Entity Diagram

Suppose we choose PASSENGER as our primary entity. PASSENGER has the following attributes: frequent flier #, name [first, middle, last], articles of luggage. We draw this much of the diagram, choosing frequent flier # as a key and noting the composite attribute, name. This diagram is shown in Figure 4.7.

Step 2: Use structured English for entities, attributes, and keys to describe the database that has been elicited.

The Entity

This database records data about PASSENGERS. For each passenger, we record the following: frequent flier #, name [first, middle, last], articles of luggage.

The Attributes

For atomic attributes, att(j):

For each PASSENGER, there always will be one and only one frequent flier #. The value for frequent flier # will not be subdivided.

For each PASSENGER, there always will be one and only one recording of articles of luggage. The value for articles of luggage will not be subdivided.

For composite attributes, att(j):

For each PASSENGER, we will record their name, which is composed of first, middle, and last. First, middle, and last are the component parts of name.

The Keys

> For each PASSENGER, we will have the following primary key: frequent flier #.

Note that we have chosen frequent flier # as a primary key for PASSENGER. If this were not true, some other means of unique identification would be necessary. Here this is all the information we are given.

Step 3: Examine attributes in the primary entity (possibly with user assistance) to find out if information about one of the attributes is to be recorded. No further information is suggested.

Step 4: If another entity is appropriate, draw the second entity with its attributes. Repeat step 2 to see if this entity should be further split into more entities.

The other entity in this problem is FLIGHT with the following attributes: flight #, destination, depart time, arrive time.
 Again, we use the structured English:

The Entity

This database records data about Flights. For each FLIGHT, we record: flight #, destination, depart time, and arrive time.

The Attributes

For atomic attributes, att(j):

> For each FLIGHT, there always will be one and only one flight#. The value for flight# will not be subdivided.
>
> For each FLIGHT, there always will be one and only one recording of destination. The value for destination will not be subdivided.
>
> For each FLIGHT, there always will be one and only one recording of depart time. The value for depart time will not be subdivided.
>
> For each FLIGHT, there always will be one and only one recording of arrive time. The value for arrive time will not be subdivided.

The Keys

> For the key(s): (b) One candidate key (strong entity):

For each FLIGHT, we will have the following primary key: flight#. We are assuming flight # is unique.

Step 5: Connect entities with relationships if relationships exist.

What Relationship Is There between Flights and Passengers?

All passengers will fly on a flight. All flights will have multiple passengers. The diagram for this problem is illustrated in Figure 4.8 and Figure 4.9. Note that we have again made a choice: we will depict one flight per passenger in this database. The specifications do not tell us whether this should be 1 or M, so we chose 1. We also chose full participation on both sides. It would seem illogical to record data about passengers who did not fly on a flight and flights where there were no passengers. But again, if the database called for storing information about potential passengers who might not book a specific flight or flights that did not involve passengers, then we would have to change the conceptual design. Figure 4.8 is good for displaying just the entities and the attributes. Figure 4.9 uses the concise form of describing attributes and also includes some steps from above and some sample data. For conceptualizing, Figure 4.8 may be used, and later converted into Figure 4.9 style for documentation. Either figure requires an accompaniment of structured English (step 6).

Step 6: State the exact nature of the relationships in structured English from all sides. For example, if a relationship is A:B::1:M, then there is a relationship from A(1) to B(M) and from B(M) back to A(1).

Pattern 1 — M:1, from the M side, full participation

x, which are recorded in the database, must be related to one and only one y. No x are related to more than one y.

   x = passenger, y = flight, relationship = fly

> Passengers, which are recorded in the database, **must** fly on one and only one flight. No passenger flies on more than one flight.

Pattern 3 — 1:M, from the 1 side, full participation

x, which are recorded in the database, must be related to many (one or more) y's.

   x = flight, y = passenger, relationship = fly

> Flights, which are recorded in the database, **must** fly many (one or more) passengers.

Attribute descriptions follow previous patterns.

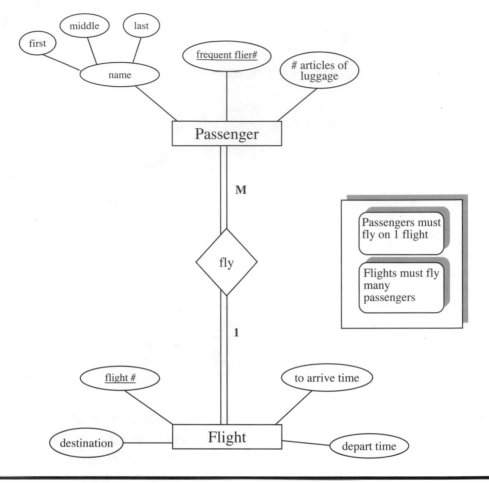

Figure 4.8   Sample Problem

Step 7: Present the "as designed" database to the user, complete with the English for entities, attributes, keys, and relationships. Refine the diagram as necessary.

Step 8: Show some sample data.

See Figure 4.9.

Mapping Relationships to a Relational Database

In this section we will continue with the mapping rules that we began at the end of Chapter 2. In Chapter 2 we learned how to map entities, entities with composite attributes, and entities with multi-valued attributes. In this chapter, having covered structural constraints of relationships, we will learn how to map relationships.

1. **Identify the entities:** Passenger, Flight

2. **Add attributes to entities, identifying primary keys**:

    Passenger (name[last, first, mi], <u>frequent flier #</u>, # articles of luggage)

    Flight (<u>flight #</u>, destination, depart time, arrive time)

3. **What relationship is there** between Passengers and Flights?

    Passengers fly on flights.

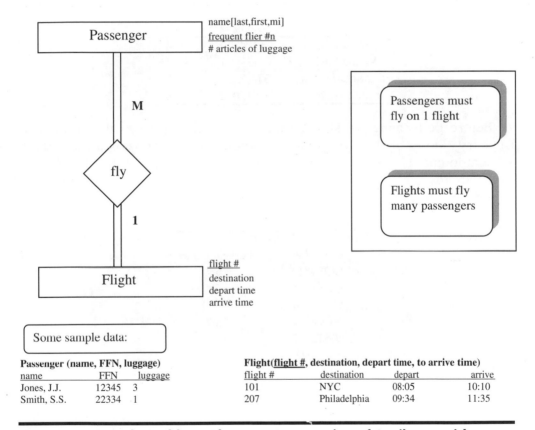

Figure 4.9   Sample Problem: Alternate Presentation of Attributes with Explanation and Sample Data

Our first mapping rule for mapping relationships maps binary M:N relationships.

> **M3a — For binary M:N relationships: For each M:N relationship, create a new table (relation) with the primary keys of each of the two entities (owner entities) that are being related in the M:N relationship. The key of this new table will be the concatenated keys of the owner entities. Include any attributes that the M:N relationship may have in this new table.**

For example, refer to Figure 4.6. If the STUDENT and COURSE tables have the following data:

		STUDENT		
name.first	*name.last*	*name.mi*	*student_number*	*address*
Richard	Earp	W	589	222 2nd St.
Boris	Backer		909	333 Dreistrasse
Helga	Hogan	H	384	88 Half Moon Ave.
Arpan	Bagui	K	876	33 Bloom Ave
Hema	Malini		505	100 Livingstone

COURSE		
cname	*c_number*	*credit_hrs*
Database	COP4710	4
Visual Basic	CGS3464	3
Elements of Stats	STA3023	3
Indian History	HIST2022	4

Before performing the M3a mapping rule, one must first insure that the primary keys of the entities involved have been established. If student_number and c_number are the primary keys of STUDENT and COURSE, respectively, then to map the M:N relationship, we create a relation called ENROLL, as follows:

ENROLL	
c_number	*student_number*
COP4710	589
CGS3464	589
CGS3464	909
STA3023	589
HIST2022	384
STA3023	505
STA3023	876
HIST2022	876
HIST2022	505

Both c_number and student_number together are the primary key of the relation, ENROLL.

Our next set of mapping rules for mapping relationships maps binary 1:1 relationships:

> **M3b — For binary 1:1 relationships: Include the primary key of EntityA into EntityB as the foreign key.**

The question is: which is EntityA and which is EntityB? This question is answered in the next three mapping rules: M3b_1, M3b_2, and M3b_3.

> **M3b_1 — For binary 1:1 relationships, if one of the sides has full participation in the relationship, and the other has partial participation, then store the primary key of the side with the partial participation constraint on the side with the full participation constraint. Include any attributes of the relationship on the side that gets the primary key (the primary key now becomes the Foreign key in the new relation).**

For example, refer to Figure 4.2. It says:

> An automobile, recorded in the database, **must** be driven by one and only one student.

and

> A student may drive one and only one automobile.

Here, the full participation is on the AUTOMOBILE side since "An automobile 'must' be driven by a student."

So we take the primary key from the partial participation side, STUDENT, and include it in the AUTOMOBILE table. The primary key of STUDENT is student_number, so this will be stored in the AUTOMOBILE relation as the foreign key. A relational database realization of the ER diagram in Figure 4.2 with some data would look like this:

AUTOMOBILE					
vehicle_id	*make*	*body_style*	*color*	*year*	*student_number*
A39583	Ford	Compact	Blue	1999	589
B83974	Chevy	Compact	Red	1989	909
E98722	Mazda	Van	Green	2002	876
F77665	Ford	Compact	White	1998	384

STUDENT				
name.first	*name.last*	*name.mi*	*student_number*	*address*
Richard	Earp	W	589	222 2nd St
Boris	Backer		909	333 Dreistrasse
Helga	Hogan	H	384	88 Half Moon Ave
Arpan	Bagui	K	876	33 Bloom Ave
Hema	Malini		505	100 Livingstone

Since STUDENT has a multi-valued attribute school, we need the table below to map the multi-valued attribute.

Name–School	
student_number	school
589	St. Helens
589	Mountain
589	Volcano
909	Manatee U
909	Everglades High
384	PCA
384	Pensacola High
876	UWF
505	Cuttington
505	UT

In this case, if the relationship had any attributes, it would be included in the relation, AUTOMOBILE.

> **M3b_2 — For binary 1:1 relationships, if both sides have partial participation constraints, there are three alternative ways to implement a relational database:**

> **M3b_2a — First alternative — you may select either one of the relations to store the key of the other (and live with some null values).**

> **M3b_2b — Second alternative — depending on the semantics of the situation, you can create a new relation to house the relationship that would contain the key of the two related entities (as is done in M3a).**

Again refer to Figure 4.1, here we assume that the participation constraints are partial from both sides, and assume that there is no school attribute. Then Figure 4.1 would read:

> An automobile may be driven by one and only one student.

and

> A student may drive one and only one automobile.

The relational realization could be [take the vehicle_id (primary key of AUTO-MOBILE) and store it in STUDENT, as shown below]:

AUTOMOBILE				
vehicle_id	make	body_style	color	year
A39583	Ford	Compact	Blue	1999
B83974	Chevy	Compact	Red	1989
E98722	Mazda	Van	Green	2002
F77665	Ford	Compact	White	1998
G99999	Chevy	Van	Grey	1989

			STUDENT		
name.first	*name.last*	*name.mi*	*student_number*	*address*	*vehicle_id*
Richard	Earp	W	589	222 2nd St	A39583
Boris	Backer		909	333 Dreistrasse	B83974
Helga	Hogan	H	384	88 Half Moon Ave	F77665
Arpan	Bagui	K	876	33 Bloom Ave	E98722
Hema	Malini		505	100 Livingstone	

In the STUDENT relation, vehicle_id is the foreign key.

M3b_2c — The third way of implementing this 1:1 binary relationship with partial participation on both sides would be to create a new table (relation) with just the keys from the two tables STUDENT and AUTOMOBILE, in addition to the two tables, STUDENT and AUTOMOBILE. In this case we would map the relations as we did in the binary M:N case; and if there were any null values, these would be left out of the linking table, as shown below:

STUDENT–AUTOMOBILE	
vehicle_id	*student_number*
A39583	589
B83974	909
E98722	876
F77665	384

In this case, the two relations STUDENT and AUTOMOBILE would remain as:

		STUDENT		
name.first	*name.last*	*name.mi*	*student_number*	*address*
Richard	Earp	W	589	222 2nd St
Boris	Backer		909	333 Dreistrasse
Helga	Hogan	H	384	88 Half Moon Ave
Arpan	Bagui	K	876	33 Bloom Ave
Hema	Malini		505	100 Livingstone

		AUTOMOBILE		
vehicle_id	*make*	*body_style*	*color*	*year*
A39583	Ford	Compact	Blue	1999
B83974	Chevy	Compact	Red	1989
E98722	Mazda	Van	Green	2002
F77665	Ford	Compact	White	1998
G99999	Chevy	Van	Grey	1989

M3b_3 — For binary 1:1 relationships, if both sides have full participation constraints, you may use the semantics of the relationship to select which of the relations should contain the key of the other. It would be inappropriate to include foreign keys in both tables as you would be introducing redundancy in the database. Include any attributes on the relationship, on the relation that is getting the foreign key.

Now assuming full participation on both sides of Figure 4.1, the two tables STUDENT and AUTOMOBILE could be:

		STUDENT		
name.first	*name.last*	*name.mi*	*student_number*	*address*
Richard	Earp	W	589	222 2nd St
Boris	Backer		909	333 Dreistrasse
Helga	Hogan	H	384	88 Half Moon Ave
Arpan	Bagui	K	876	33 Bloom Ave
Hema	Malini		505	100 Livingstone

		AUTOMOBILE			
vehicle_id	*make*	*body_style*	*color*	*year*	*student_number*
A39583	Ford	Compact	Blue	1999	589
B83974	Chevy	Compact	Red	1989	909
E98722	Mazda	Van	Green	2002	876
F77665	Ford	Compact	White	1998	384
G99999	Chevy	Van	Grey	1989	505

In this above case, the student_number was included in AUTOMOBILE, making student_number a foreign key in AUTOMOBILE. We could have also taken the primary key from AUTOMOBILE, vehicle_id, and included that in STUDENT table.

In this case, if the relationship had any attributes, these would have been stored in AUTOMOBILE, along with student_number.

The next set of mapping relationships maps binary 1:N relationships:

> **M3c — For binary 1:N relationships, we have to check what kind of participation constraints the N side of the relationship has:**

> **M3c_1 — For binary 1:N relationships, if the N-side has full participation, include the key of the entity from the 1 side, in the relation on the N side as a foreign key.**

For example, in Figure 4.4 if we assume full participation on the student side, we will have:

Dorm rooms may have zero or more students.

and

Students must live in one and only one dorm room.

The relational realization would be:

STUDENT				
name.first	*name.last*	*name.mi*	*student_number*	*dorm*
Richard	Earp	W	589	A
Boris	Backer		909	C
Helga	Hogan	H	384	A
Arpan	Bagui	K	876	A
Hema	Malini		505	B

DORM	
dname	*supervisor*
A	Saunders
B	Backer
C	Hogan
D	Eisenhower

Here, the full participation is on the N side, that is, on the STUDENT entity side. So, we take the key from DORM, dname, and include it in the STUDENT relation. In this case, if the relationship had an attribute, it would be included in STUDENT, the N side.

> **M3c_2 — For binary 1:N relationships, if the N-side has partial participation, the 1:N relationship is handled just like a binary M:N relationship with a separate table for the relationship. The key of the new relation consists of a concatenation of the keys of the related entities. Include any attributes that were on the relationship, on this new table.**

Checkpoint 4.4

1. State the mapping rules that would be used to map Figure 4.5? Map Figure 4.5 to a relational database and show some sample data.
2. State the mapping rules that would be used to map Figure 4.8? Map Figure 4.8 to a relational database and show some sample data.

Chapter Summary

This chapter discussed cardinality and participation ratios in ER diagrams. Several examples and diagrams of binary relationships with structural constraints (developed in the Chen-like model) were discussed. Tighter English grammar was presented for each of the diagrams, and steps 7 and 8 of the ER design methodology were defined. The final section of the chapter discussed mapping relationships.

Chapter 4 Exercises

Exercise 4.1

Refer to Figure 2.3. Suppose that the only attributes of STUDENT are student number and name. And, let us suppose that we have another entity called "high school," which is going to be the high school from which the student graduated. For the high school entity, we will record the high school name and the location (meaning city and state). Draw the ER diagrams using the Chen-like model. Follow the methodology and include all English descriptions of your diagrams. Map the ER diagrams to a relational database.

Exercise 4.2

Suppose that a college has one dormitory with many rooms. The dormitory entity, which is actually a "dormitory room" entity because there is only one dorm, has the attributes room number and single/double (meaning that there are private rooms and double rooms). Let us suppose that the STUDENT entity in this case contains the attributes student number, student name, and home telephone number. Draw the ER diagrams using the Chen-like model. Follow the methodology and include all English descriptions of your diagrams. Map the ER diagrams to a relational database.

Exercise 4.3

Consider a student database with students and campus organizations. Students will have the attributes of student number and student name. Organizations will have the following attributes: organization name and organization type. Draw the ER diagrams using the Chen-like model. Follow the methodology and include all English descriptions of your diagrams. Map the ER diagram to a relational database and include some sample data.

Exercise 4.4

Consider a student and advisor database. Students have a student number and student name. Advisors have names, office numbers, and advise in some major. The major that the advisor advises in is designated by a major code (e.g., Chemistry, CHEM; Biology, BIOL; Computer Science, COMPSC: etc.) Draw the ER diagrams using the Chen-like model. Follow the methodology and include all English descriptions of your diagrams. Map the ER diagram to a relational database and include some sample data.

Exercise 4.5

You want to record the following data in a database: restaurant name and location, employee names and IDs, capacity of restaurant (smoking and non-smoking),

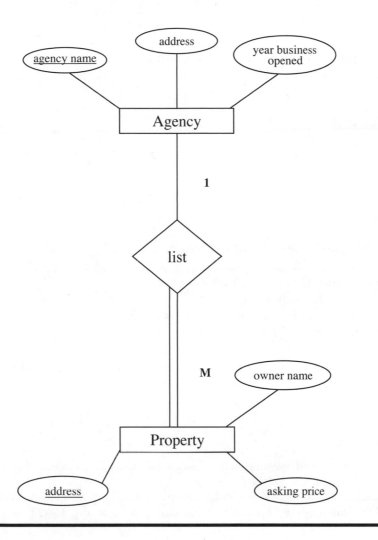

Figure 4.10

hours of operation (assume same hours every day), employee salaries and titles. An employee can work for only one restaurant. Draw the ER diagrams using the Chen-like model. Follow the methodology and include all English descriptions of your diagrams. Map the ER diagram to a relational database and include some sample data.

Exercise 4.6

Record the following data in a database: business name, owner, location(s), telephone #(s), delivery truck number, truck capacity, usual route description (e.g., North, West, Central, Lake). Draw the ER diagrams using the Chen-like model. Follow the methodology and include all English descriptions of your diagrams.

Exercise 4.7

Refer to Figure 4.10. What are the English language statements you can make about the figure?

Exercise 4.8

Refer to Figure 4.9. Complete the diagram by adding a precise English description of each attribute. Map Figure 4.9 to a relational database.

Exercise 4.9

What is the cardinality of the following?

    a. Each student can have only one car
    b. Each student has many cars
    c. Each car can be driven by many students
    d. Each car must be driven by many students.

Which of these above cardinality rules are optional? Which rules are mandatory? Diagramatically show these relationships.

References

Batani, C., Ceri, S., and Navathe, S.B., *Conceptual Database Design,* Benjamin/Cummings Publishing, Redwood City, CA, 1992.

Earp, R. and Bagui, S., "Extending Relationships in the Entity Relationship Diagram," *Data Base Management,* Auerbach Publications, Boca Raton, FL, 22-10-42, 1–14, May 2001.

Elmasri, R. and Navathe, S.B., *Fundamentals of Database Systems,* 3rd ed., Addison-Wesley, Reading, MA, 2000.

Kroenke, D.M., *Database Processing,* Prentice Hall, Upper Saddle River, NJ, 2000.

McFadden, F.R. and Hoffer, J.A., *Modern Database Management,* 4th ed., Benjamin/ Cummings Publishing, Redwood City, CA, 1994.

Ramakrishnan, R. and Gehrke, J., *Database Management Systems,* 3rd ed., McGraw-Hill, New York, 2003.

Sanders, L., *Data Modeling,* Boyd & Fraser Publishing, Danvers, MA, 1995.

Case Study:
West Florida Mall (continued)

In the past few chapters we selected our primary entities (as per the specifications from the user so far) and defined the relationships between the primary entities. In this chapter we proceed with the ER diagram for this case study by looking at steps 6 and 7 of the ER design methodology, and map the ER diagram to a relational database (with some sample data) as we proceed.

Step 6 develops the structural constraints of binary relationships by stating:

Step 6: State the exact nature of the relationships in structured English from all sides. For Example, if a relationship is A:B::1:M, then there is a relationship from A(1) to B(M) and from B(M) back to A(1).

Refer to Figure 4.11.

First, for the relationship located_in:

From MALL to STORE, this fits Pattern 3, **1(full):N**:

> One mall must have many (at least one) stores.

or

> Malls, which are recorded in the database, must have many (one or more) stores located in them.

From STORE to MALL, this fits Pattern 1, **M(full):1**:

> Many stores (one or more) must be in one mall.

or

> Stores, which are recorded in the database, must be in one mall.

To map this relationship (with some sample data):

The MALL entity will be mapped as was shown in the case study in Chapters 2 and 3 (as shown on the following page):

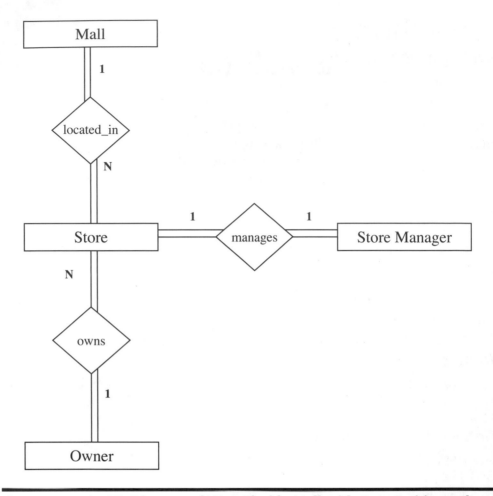

Figure 4.11   An ER Diagram of West Florida Mall with Four Entities and Structural Constraints

MALL–Store	
name	*store_name*
West Florida Mall	Penney's
West Florida Mall	Sears
West Florida Mall	Dollar Store
West Florida Mall	Rex
Cordova Mall	Dillards
.	
.	
.	

MALL	
name	*address*
West Florida Mall	N Davis Hwy, Pensacola, FL
Cordova Mall	9th Avenue, Pensacola, FL
Navy Mall	Navy Blvd, Pensacola, FL
BelAir Mall	10th Avenue, Mobile, AL

Next, we have to map the relationship between the MALL entity and the STORE entity. This is a binary 1:N relationship; hence, we will use mapping rule M3c_1, which states:

M3c_1 — For binary 1:N relationships, if the N-side has full participation, include the key of the entity from the 1 side, in the relation on the N side as a foreign key.

So, the key from the 1 side, the MALL side, name (meaning, mall_name), will be included in the N side, STORE side, as the foreign key, as follows:

	STORE		
sloc	*sname*	*snum*	*mall_name*
Rm 101	Penney's	1	West Florida Mall
Rm 102	Sears	2	West Florida Mall
Rm 109	Dollar Store	3	West Florida Mall
Rm 110	Rex	4	West Florida Mall

Due to the multi-valued attribute, depts, in STORE, we will keep the relation with the multi-valued attribute (as developed in Chapter 3):

	STORE–dept
snum	*depts*
1	Tall men's clothing
1	Women's clothing
1	Children's clothing
1	Men's clothing
.	
.	
.	

Then, for the relationship owns:

From OWNER to STORE, this fits Pattern 3, **1(full):M**:

Owners, which are recorded in the database, must own one or more stores.

or

One owner must own at least one store, and may own many stores.

From STORE to OWNER, this fits Pattern 1, **M(full):1**:

Stores, which are recorded in the database, must have one and only one owner.

or

Many stores can have one owner.

To map this relationship (with some sample data):

For the relationship owns, from OWNER to STORE, a **1:N** relationship:
    Again, using mapping rule M3c_1, we will take the key from the 1 side, so_ssn, and include this as the foreign key in the N side, STORE, so STORE now becomes:

		STORE		
sloc	*sname*	*snum*	*mall_name*	*so_ssn*
Rm 101	Penney's	1	West Florida Mall	879–987–0987
Rm 102	Sears	2	West Florida Mall	928–088–7654
Rm 109	Dollar Store	3	West Florida Mall	826–098–0877
Rm 110	Rex	4	West Florida Mall	982–876–8766

And the relation for the OWNER entity remains as developed in the earlier chapter:

		OWNER	
so_ssn	*so_name*	*so_off_phone*	*so_address*
879–987–0987	Earp	(850)474–2093	1195 Gulf Breeze Pkwy, Pensacola, FL
826–098–0877	Sardar	(850)474–9873	109 Navy Blvd, Pensacola, FL
928–088–7654	Bagui	(850)474–9382	89 Highland Heights, Tampa, FL
982–876–8766	Bush	(850)474–9283	987 Middle Tree, Mobile, AL

Next, for the relationship, manages:

From STORE to STORE MANAGER, this fits Pattern 1, **1(full):1**:

Stores, which are recorded in the database, must have one store manager.

or

Stores must have one store manager, and can only have one and only store manager.

From STORE MANAGER to STORE, this also fits Pattern 1, **1(full):1**:

Store managers, which are recorded in the database, must manage one and only one store.

or

Store managers must manage at least one store, and can manage only one store.

To map this relationship (with some sample data):

The relationship between STORE and STORE MANAGER is a binary 1:1 relationship, hence using mapping rule M3b_3, the relation STORE would develop into (we are taking the key from STORE MANAGER, sm_ssn, and including it in STORE as the foreign key):

			STORE		
sloc	*sname*	*snum*	*mall_name*	*so_ssn*	*sm_ssn*
Rm 101	Penney's	1	West Florida Mall	879–987–0987	283–972–0927
Rm 102	Sears	2	West Florida Mall	928–088–7654	456–098–0987
Rm 109	Dollar Store	3	West Florida Mall	826–098–0877	234–987–0988
Rm 110	Rex	4	West Florida Mall	982–876–8766	928–982–9882

And the relation for the STORE MANAGER entity remains as was developed in the earlier chapter:

	STORE MANAGER	
sm_ssn	*sm_name*	*sm_salary*
234–987–0988	Saha	45,900
456–098–0987	Becker	43,989
928–982–9882	Ford	44,000
283–972–0927	Raja	38,988

Our next step will be step 7, which is:

Step 7: Present the "as-designed" database to the user, complete with the English for entities, attributes, keys, and relationships. Refine the diagram as necessary.

In summary our relational database has so far been mapped to (without the data):
(Note: The primary keys are underlined.)

MALL–Store

name	store_name

MALL

name	address

STORE

sloc	sname	snum	mall_name	so_ssn	sm_ssn

STORE–dept

snum	depts

OWNER

so_ssn	so_name	so_off_phone	so_address

STORE MANAGER

sm_ssn	sm_name	sm_salary

We continue with the development of this case study at the end of Chapter 5.

The Weak Entity

Chapter Topics

Chapters 2 and 3 introduced the concepts of the entity, the attribute, and the relationship. Chapter 4 dealt with structural constraints, that is, how two entities are related to one another. This chapter discusses the concept of the "weak" entity, which is used in the Chen-like model. Weak entities may not have a key attribute of their own, as they are dependent on a strong or regular entity for their existence (that has a key attribute of its own). The weak entity has some restrictions on its use, and produces some interesting diagrams. This chapter revisits and redefines steps 3 and 4 of the ER design methodology to include the concept of the weak entity. A grammar for the weak entities and mapping rules for the weak entities are also developed.

Strong and Weak Entities

As discussed in Chapter 2, there are situations where finding a key to a relationship is difficult. So far, we have concentrated on examples with strong (regular) entities — mostly ones with easily identifiable keys. Strong entities almost always have a unique identifier that is a subset of all the attributes; a unique identifier may be an attribute or a group of attributes. For example, a student number, an automobile vehicle identification number, a driving license number, etc. may be unique identifiers of strong entities.

A weak entity is one that clearly will be an entity but will depend on another entity for its existence. As previously mentioned, a weak entity will not necessarily have a unique identifier. A classic example of this kind of entity is a DEPENDENT as related to an EMPLOYEE entity. If one were constructing a database about employees and their dependents, an instance of a dependent would depend entirely on some instance of an employee, or else the dependent would not be kept in the database. The EMPLOYEE entity is called the *owner* entity or *identifying* entity for the weak entity DEPENDENT.

How can a weak entity come about in our diagrams? In the creation of a database, we might have a dependent name shown as a multi-valued attribute, as shown in Figure 5.1. An example of data for a diagram like Figure 5.1 would be:

name (First, MI, Last)	EMPLOYEE emp ID	dependents
John J. Jones	0001	John, Jr; Fred; Sally
Sam S. Smith	0004	Brenda; Richard
Adam A. Adams	0007	John; Quincy; Maude
Santosh P. Saha	0009	Ranu; Pradeep; Mala

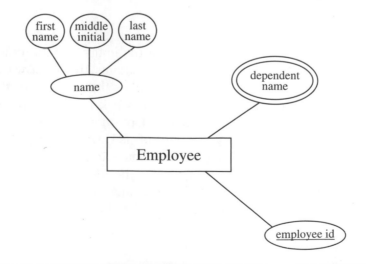

Figure 5.1   The EMPLOYEE Entity Showing DEPENDENT Name as a Multi-Valued Attribute

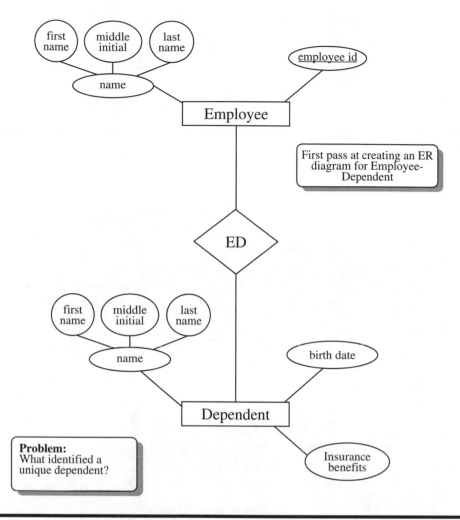

Figure 5.2 The EMPLOYEE–DEPENDENT ER Diagram — First Pass

Suppose that in our conversations with the user, we discover that more information is supposed to be gathered about the dependents themselves. Following our methodology, this acknowledgment is a recognition that the dependents should be entities; that is, they fit the criteria for "entity," which is that we would be recording information about "something" (the dependent). Hence, we would be describing an entity called DEPENDENT. If we make DEPENDENT an entity, we would embellish the diagram in Figure 5.1 to that of Figure 5.2.

Figure 5.2 poses a problem: the DEPENDENT entity is dependent on the EMPLOYEE for its being. Also, it has no clear unique identifier. This dependence on EMPLOYEE makes DEPENDENT a weak entity. As is often the case with weak entities, neither name, birth date, nor insurance benefits are candidate keys by themselves. None of these attributes would have unique values. There is no single attribute candidate key.

In the Chen-like model, for weak entities, we enclose the entity in a double box, and the corresponding relationship to the owner in a double diamond

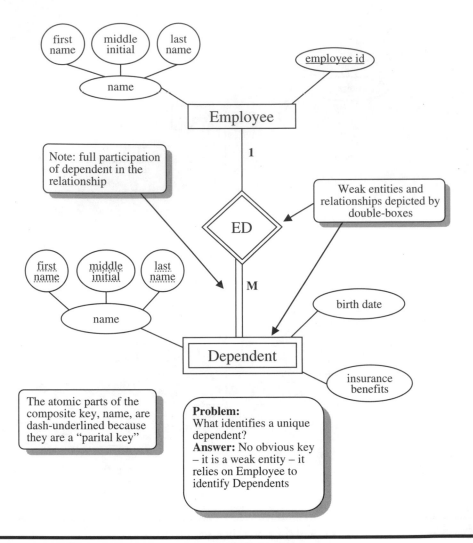

Figure 5.3   The EMPLOYEE–DEPENDENT ER Diagram

(see Figure 5.3). The weak entity in Figure 5.3, the DEPENDENT, is said to be identified by the entity EMPLOYEE; the EMPLOYEE is called the "identifying entity" or "owner entity" for the weak entity, DEPENDENT.

Attributes are handled the same way for weak entities as for strong entities (except that there may be no primary keys for weak entities). We have included some attributes in Figure 5.3 so that the figures depict the following (in loose grammar):

A dependent must be related to one employee and an employee may have many dependents.

The DEPENDENT entity has the following attributes: name (a composite attribute), birth date, and insurance benefits.

In dealing with weak entities, it is appropriate to consider how each instance of the entity would be identified. Because the owner of the weak entity, DEPENDENT, is the strong entity EMPLOYEE, the identification process would involve the EMPLOYEE key plus some information from the weak entity, DEPENDENT. Name is a likely candidate as an identifier for DEPENDENT, and will be called a *partial key*.

In Figure 5.3, we have dash-underlined the atomic parts of the composite attribute, name. Name is a *partial key* as it identifies dependents, but not uniquely. Because name is composite, the atomic parts of it are distinguished as the partial key. This assumes that all dependents have unique names.

In Figure 5.3, we did not "name" the relationship, and left it as *ED* for EMPLOYEE-DEPENDENT. Suitable names for the dependent might be "have," as in:

Employees may **have** many dependents.

or "dependent upon" as in

Employees may **have** many dependents **dependent upon** them.

We could also have used "related to," as in:

Employees are related to many dependents.

Each of these verb phrases seems to have a redundancy (dependent upon) or perhaps misleading (related to) air about them. Probably the best thing to do there is to leave the relationship unnamed (*ED*).

Weak Entities and Structural Constraints

Weak entities always have full or mandatory participation from the weak side toward the owner. If the weak entity does not have total participation, then we would have a data item in the database that is not uniquely identified, and which is not tied to a strong entity. In our EMPLOYEE–DEPENDENT example, this would be like keeping track of a dependent that is not related in any way to an employee. The cardinality of the relationship between the weak and strong entity will usually be 1:M, but not necessarily so.

Weak Entities and the Identifying Owner

There are situations in which a weak entity can be connected to an owner entity while other relationships exist apart from the "owner" relationship. For example, consider Figure 5.4. In this figure, we have shown two relationships — *owns* and *drives* — connecting the two entities, EMPLOYEE and AUTOMOBILE. Here, the AUTOMOBILE entity is considered a weak

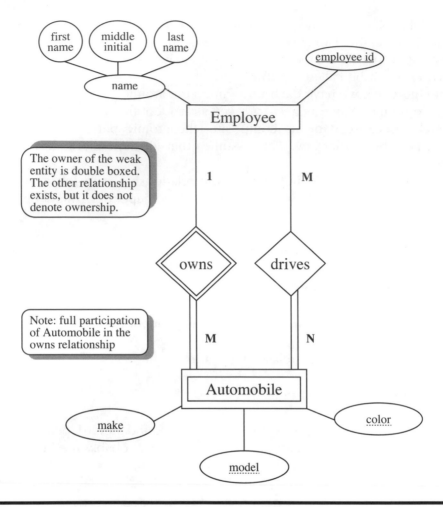

Figure 5.4   A Weak Entity with Two Relationships

entity; that is, if there is no employee, then there will be no automobile (the automobile has to have an employee to exist in the database). Further, the automobile is identified by the owner; note the double diamond on the *owns* relationship, and the full participation of the AUTOMOBILE entity in the *owns* relationship.

In Figure 5.4, we also have a *drives* relationship. The automobile is driven by employees other than the owner. All automobiles are driven by some employee and, hence, the participation is full. However, the driver-employee may not necessarily be the actual owner. To identify AUTOMO-BILE we are saying that we need the *owns* relationship, but other non-owner drivers may exist.

According to Figure 5.4, one employee may own many automobiles. To answer the question — which automobiles does an employee own, in addition to the employee's_id, we will need to know the make, model, and color of the automobiles. The make, model, and color of the AUTOMOBILE entity are partial keys (dotted underline in Figure 5.4).

Checkpoint 5.1

1. How would you identify a strong entity?
2. How would you identify a weak entity?
3. What kind of a relationship line (single or double) would be leading up to the weak entity in a Chen-like diagram?
4. What kind of relationship does a weak entity have in a Chen-like model?
5. What is a partial key?

Another Example of a Weak Entity and the Identifying Owner

As another example of a weak entity and the identifying owner in an ER diagram, consider Figure 5.5. In this figure we have two strong entities: PERSON and VET. There is one weak entity, PET. Figure 5.5 illustrates that PERSON *owns* PET, but the VET *treats* the PET. In this diagram, PERSON is the identifying or controlling entity for PET and, hence, the relationship *owns* has a double diamond. The relationship *owns* is a weak relationship. PET is a weak entity with respect to PERSON.

Conversely, the relationship *treats* does not have a double diamond because VET is not the owner of PET. Here, *treats* is not a weak relationship, and PET is not a weak entity with respect to VET.

Weak Entities Connected to Other Weak Entities

A final point regarding weak entities. Just because an entity is weak does not preclude it from being an owner of another weak entity. For example, consider Figure 5.6. In this figure, the EMPLOYEE–DEPENDENT relationship has been enhanced to include hobbies of the dependents. (Never mind why one would want to keep this information, but let us suppose that they do anyway).

DEPENDENT is a weak entity. The entity HOBBY is also weak. Hobbies might be identified by their type (e.g., stamp collecting, baseball, tying knots, observing trains, etc.). The type attribute of HOBBY is a partial key for HOBBY.

The entity DEPENDENT is the owner of the entity HOBBY, and the entity EMPLOYEE is the owner of the weak entity DEPENDENT.

The reason that this situation is brought up here is to show that it can exist. Later, when we map this situation, we will treat this special situation carefully.

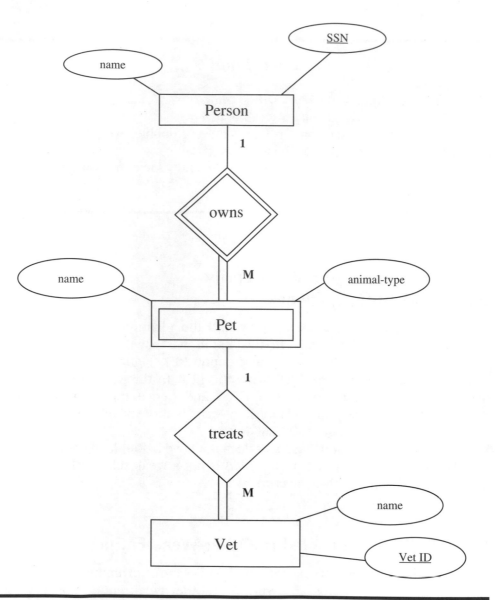

Figure 5.5   The PERSON–PET–VET ER Diagram

Checkpoint 5.2

1. Can a weak entity be dependent on another weak entity?
2. Can a weak entity have a relationship that is not "weak" with the identifying entity?
3. Can a weak entity be related to more than one entity (strong or weak)?

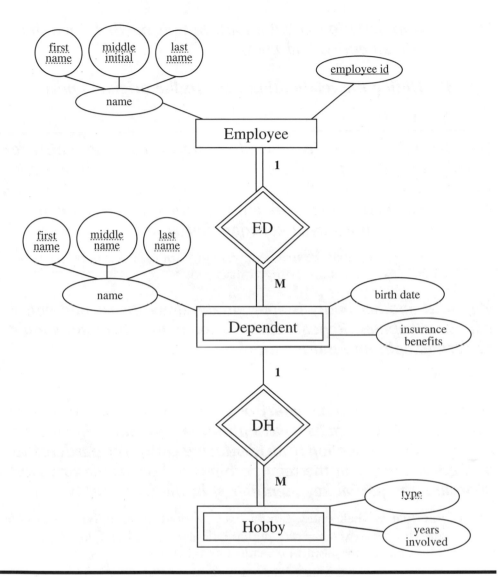

Figure 5.6   The EMPLOYEE–DEPENDENT–HOBBY ER Diagram

Revisiting the Methodology

The inclusion of a weak entity in an ER diagram causes us to again look at our methodology and make some adjustments. We might discover the weak entity in one of two places: one would be as we illustrated with the evolution of the multi-valued attribute, the "dependent"; this would occur in step 3a and 3b:

Step 3: Examine attributes in the primary entity (possibly with user assistance) to find out if information about one of the attributes is to be recorded.

Step 3a: If information about an attribute is needed, then make the attribute an entity, and then

Step 3b: Define the relationship back to the original entity.

So we add:

Step 3c: If the new entity depends entirely on another entity for its existence, then draw the entity as weak (double boxed) and show the connection to the identifying entity as a double diamond. The participation of the weak entity in the relationship is full. Dash-underline the partial key identifier(s) in the weak entity.

The second place that a weak entity might appear would be as part of step 4 when new entities are being considered:

Step 4: If another entity is appropriate, draw the second entity with its attributes. Repeat step 2 to see if any attributes should be further split into more entities.

So we add:

Step 4a: If the additional entity or entities do not have candidate keys, then draw them as weak entities (as explained in step 3c) and show the connection to an identifying entity. The participation of the weak entity in the relationship is full or mandatory. Dash-underline the partial key identifier(s) in the weak entity.

Again, note that a weak entity cannot exist without an identifying entity. So if the weak entity is "discovered" independent of an identifying entity, the relationship-connection should be made immediately.

Weak Entity Grammar

We previously discussed some grammar associated with weak entities, but now we want to revise and enhance the idea when we have no primary key for the weak entity. It is possible for a weak entity to have a primary key and therefore it might appear in item (b), so we add part (c).

The Keys

For the key(s):
(a) More than one candidate key (strong entity): ... [discussed previously]
(b) One candidate key (strong or weak entity): For each weak entity, but it is assumed that no weak entity will be recorded without a corresponding owner (strong) entity. [discussed previously]

(c) No candidate keys (weak entity): For each *(weak) Entity*, we do not assume that any attribute will be unique enough to identify individual entities.

In this case, the DEPENDENT entity would be depicted as:

For each DEPENDENT entity, we do not assume that any attribute will be unique enough to identify individual entities.

We will now enhance this description to include the identifying entity: Because the *weak entity* does not have a candidate key, each *weak entity* will be identified by key(s) belonging to the *strong entity*.

In this case, the DEPENDENT entity is identified by the EMPLOYEE entity and this second statement becomes:

Because the DEPENDENT entity does not have a candidate key, each DEPENDENT entity will be identified by key(s) belonging to the EMPLOYEE entity, plus name (the partial key) in the DEPENDENT entity.

Mapping Weak Entities to a Relational Database

In this section we develop the mapping rules for mapping weak entities to a relational database.

M4 — For weak entities — Develop a new table (relation) for each weak entity. As is the case with the strong entity, include any atomic attributes from the weak entity in the table. If there is a composite attribute, include only the atomic parts of the composite attribute, and be sure to qualify the atomic parts in order to not lose information. To relate the weak entity to its owner, include the primary key of the owner entity in the weak relation as a foreign key. The primary key of the weak relation will be the partial key in the weak entity concatenated to the key of the owner entity.

If weak entities own other weak entities, then the weak entity that is connected to the strong entity must be mapped first. The key of the weak owner entity has to be defined before the "weaker" entity (the one furthest from the strong entity) can be mapped.

For example, refer to Figure 5.3. The EMPLOYEE relation and DEPENDENT relation would be mapped as shown below:

EMPLOYEE			
ename.first	ename.last	ename.mi	employee_id
Richard	Earp	W	589
Boris	Backer		909
Helga	Hogan	H	384
Arpan	Bagui	K	876
Hema	Malini		505

(employee_id is the primary key of EMPLOYEE).

		DEPENDENT			
dname.first	*dname.last*	*dname.mi*	*birth_date*	*insurance*	*employee_id*
Beryl	Earp	W	1/1/74	SE	589
Kaitlyn	Backer		2/25/78	SE	909
David	Earp	H	3/4/75	BlueCross	589
Fred	Earp	K	3/7/98	BlueCross	589
Chloe	Hogan		5/6/88	SE	384

The primary key, employee_id, from the owner relation, EMPLOYEE, is included in the weak entity, DEPENDENT. employee_id now becomes part of the primary key of DEPENDENT. Because dname.first, dname.last, and dname.mi are the partial key of the DEPENDENT relation, the primary key of the DEPENDENT relation now finally becomes dname.first, dname.last, dname.mi, and employee_id all together.

Now refer to Figure 5.6. Here, the DEPENDENT relation is dependent on the EMPLOYEE relation, and the HOBBY relation is dependent on the DEPENDENT relation. The EMPLOYEE relation and DEPENDENT relation would be mapped as shown above, and then the HOBBY relation would be mapped as shown below:

		HOBBY			
dname.first	*dname.last*	*dname.mi*	*employee_id*	*type*	*years_involved*
Beryl	Earp	W	589	swimming	3
Kaitlyn	Backer		909	reading	5
David	Earp	H	589	hiking	1
Fred	Earp	K	589	fishing	2
Chloe	Hogan		384	singing	4

The partial key of HOBBY was type. The primary key of the HOBBY relation now becomes dname.first, dname.last, dname.mi, employee_id, and type, all together.

Checkpoint 5.3

1. What are the rules for mapping weak entities? Map Figure 5.5 and show some sample data.
2. When mapping weak entities, what becomes their new primary key?
3. How would you map multi-valued attributes in a weak entity? Discuss.

Chapter Summary

This chapter discussed and developed the concept of the "weak entity." The grammar for the weak entity was enhanced, along with the ER design methodology. The mapping rules for mapping the weak entity were also developed. This concept of the weak entity is available in the Chen-like model but is treated differently in many other ER diagram models.

Chapter 5 Exercises

Exercise 5.1

Construct an ER diagram (in the Chen-like model) for a database that is to contain the following: employee name (ename), employee number (enum), employee address (eaddr), skill(s) (eskill). An employee may have more than one skill. Then enhance the diagram to include: level of skill, date skill certified (if certified), and date began using the skill. Are there any weak entities in this database? Map this ER diagram to a relational database.

Exercise 5.2

Construct an ER diagram (in the Chen-like model) for sports and players. Attributes of SPORTS are: sport name — type of sport — timed or untimed. Attributes of PLAYERS are: name, person ID, date of birth. Players may play multiple sports. Which entity or entities would you consider weak? Write out the grammar for the ER diagram. Map this ER diagram to a relational database.

Exercise 5.3

How are weak entities generally identified?

Exercise 5.4

What mapping rules would be used to map Figure 5.4? Map Figure 5.4 to a relational database and show some sample data.

References

Chen, P.P., "The Entity Relationship Model — Toward a Unified View of Data," *ACM TODS 1*, No. 1, March 1976.

Connolly, T., Begg, C., and Strachan, A., *Database Systems, A Practical Approach to Design, Implementation, and Management,* Addison-Wesley, Harlow, England, 1998.

Elmasri, R. and Navathe, S.B., *Fundamentals of Database Systems,* 3rd ed., Addison-Wesley, Reading, MA, 2000.

Ramakrishnan, R. and Gehrke, J., *Database Management Systems,* 3rd ed., McGraw-Hill, New York, 2003.

Case Study:
West Florida Mall (continued)

In the previous chapters we selected our primary entities, defined the attributes and relationships for this case study, and mapped it to a relational database (with some sample data). In Chapter 4 we also determined the structural constraints of the relationships and adjusted some of the mappings accordingly. Then we reviewed step 7, which says:

Step 7: Present the "as-designed" database to the user, complete with the English for entities, attributes, keys, and relationships. Refine the diagram as necessary.

Suppose we got some additional input from the user: A store must have one or more departments. A department will not exist without a store. For each department we will store the department name, department number, and department manager. Each department has at least one employee working for it.

We have to record information about the employees in the store. For each employee in a store, we will have to keep an employee's name, social security number, and the department in which that the employee works. Employees must work in one and only one department.

In Chapter 3 we determined that departments was a multi-valued attribute of STORE (that is, one store had many departments). But, upon reviewing these additional (above) specifications, we can now see that DEPARTMENT needs to be an entity on its own because we have to record information about a DEPARTMENT. Also, we can see that we have to record information about another new entity, EMPLOYEE. So, these above specifications add two new entities: DEPARTMENT and EMPLOYEE.

First we will select an entity, DEPARTMENT. Now, repeating Step 2 for DEPARTMENT:

The Entity

> This database records data about a DEPARTMENT. For each DEPARTMENT in the database, we record a department name (dname) and department number (dnum).

The Attributes for DEPARTMENT

> For each DEPARTMENT, there will always be one and only one dname. The value for dname will not be subdivided.

For each DEPARTMENT, there will always be one and only one dnum. The value for dnum will not be subdivided.

The Keys

For each DEPARTMENT, we do not assume that any attribute will be unique enough to identify individual entities without the accompanying reference to STORE, the owner entity. Note that the language leads you to thinking of DEPARTMENT as a weak entity.

Next, we will select our next entity, EMPLOYEE. Now, repeating step 2 for EMPLOYEE:

The Entity

This database records data about an EMPLOYEE. For each EMPLOYEE in the database, we record an employee name (ename) and employee social security number (essn).

The Attributes for EMPLOYEE

For each EMPLOYEE, there will always be one and only one ename recorded for each EMPLOYEE. The value for ename will not be subdivided.

For each EMPLOYEE, there will always be one and only one essn recorded for each EMPLOYEE. The value for essn will not be subdivided.

The Keys

For each EMPLOYEE, we will assume that the essn will be unique. (So, EMPLOYEE will be a strong entity.)

These entities have been added to the diagram in Figure 5.7.

Using step 6 to determine the structural constraints of the relationships, we get:

First, for the relationship, *dept_of*:
From STORE to DEPARTMENT, this fits Pattern 3, 1(full):N:

Stores, which are recorded in the database, must have many (one or more) departments.

From DEPARTMENT to STORE, this fits Pattern 1, M(full):1:

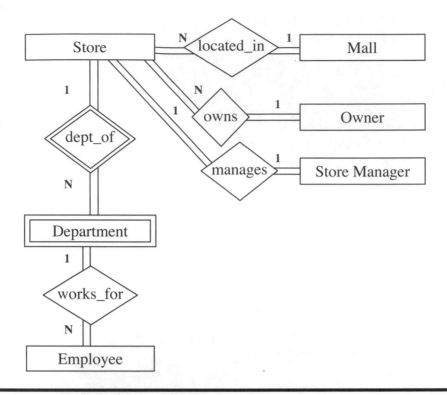

Figure 5.7   An ER Diagram of West Florida Mall Developed Thus Far

Many departments (one or more) must be in one store.

To map this relationship (with some sample data):
The relationship between STORE and DEPARTMENT is a binary 1:N relationship, so using mapping rule M3c_1, we will take the key from the 1 side, snum, and include this as the foreign key in the N side, DEPARTMENT, so the relation DEPARTMENT becomes:

DEPARTMENT		
dname	dnum	snum
Tall Men's Clothing	501	1
Men's Clothing	502	1
Women's Clothing	503	1
Children's Clothing	504	1
Men's Clothing	601	2

The STORE relation will be the same as it was in Chapter 4, but we will not need the relation, STORE_depts. (In Chapter 4, departments was still a multi valued attribute of STORE, so we had the relations STORE and STORE_depts.) From the specifications at the beginning of the case study in this chapter, it is apparent that DEPARTMENT is an entity on its own, so the STORE_depts relation is included in (replaced by) the DEPARTMENT relation.

Then, for the relationship, *works_for*:

From EMPLOYEE to DEPARTMENT, this fits Pattern 1, 1(full):1 :

Employees, who are recorded in the database, must work for one and only one department.

From DEPARTMENT to EMPLOYEE, this fits Pattern 3, 1(full):N :

Departments, which are recorded in the database, must have one or more employees working for it.

To map this relationship (with some sample data):

From EMPLOYEE to DEPARTMENT, the relationship is 1:1, and because both sides have full participation, using mapping rule M3b_3, we can select which side can store the key of the other. But, because the relationship between DEPARTMENT and EMPLOYEE is a binary 1(full):N relationship, using mapping rule M3c_1, we will take the key from the 1 side (DEPARTMENT side), dnum, and snum, and include this concatenated key as the foreign key in the N side, (EMPLOYEE side), so the relation EMPLOYEE becomes:

	EMPLOYEE		
ename	*essn*	*dnum*	*snum*
Kaitlyn	987–754–9865	501	1
Fred	276–263–91827	502	1
Katie	982–928–2726	503	1
Seema	837–937–9373	501	1
Raju	988–876–3434	601	2
.			
.			
.			

In summary, our relational database has so far been mapped to (without the data):

MALL-Store

name	store_name

MALL

name	address

STORE

sloc	sname	snum	mall_name	so_owner	sm_ssn

OWNER

so_ssn	so_name	so_off_phone	so_address

STORE MANAGER

sm_ssn	sm_name	salary

DEPARTMENT

dname	dnum	snum

EMPLOYEE

ename	essn	dnum	snum

We continue with the development of this case study at the end of Chapter 6.

Chapter 6

Further Extensions for ER Diagrams with Binary Relationships

Chapter Topics

Having developed the basic ER model in Chapters 1 through 4, this chapter deals with some extensions to the basic model. In this chapter we introduce a new concept — attributes of relationships — and give several examples of attributes of relationships. We then revisit step 6 of the ER design methodology to include attributes of relationships. Next, the chapter looks at how more entities and relationships are added to the ER model, and how attributes and relationships evolve into entities, all the while refining our ER design methodology. Relationships can develop into entities, creating an intersection entity. The grammar and structured English for the intersection entity are also presented. Then, this chapter introduces the concept of recursive relationships.

Also, in previous chapters, we only looked at cases where two entities had a (one) relationship between them. In this chapter we discuss how two entities can have more than one relationship between them. Step 5 of the ER design methodology is also redefined to include more than one relationship between two entities. This chapter discusses derived and redundant relationships, and the ER design methodology is once again refined and step 6(b) is included to deal with derived and redundant relationships. Finally, toward the conclusion of this chapter we included an optional section that looks at an alternative ER notation for specifying structural constraints on relationships.

Attributes of Relationships

In Chapter 3 we considered the M:N relationship STUDENT–COURSE. This relationship is M:N because students take many courses and courses are taken by many students. Now consider adding the attribute grade to the ER diagram. If we tried to put grade with the STUDENT entity, we would have a multi-valued attribute that had to be somehow related to the COURSE entity to make sense. Similarly, if we tried to put the grade attribute with the COURSE entity, the COURSE entity would have to be related to the STUDENT entity. The correct place for the grade attribute in the diagram would be on the relationship, enroll, because grade requires both a STUDENT and a COURSE to make sense. See Figure 6.1 for the placement of the attribute grade in an M:N, full:full participation model.

A few other attributes have been added to Figure 6.1 to show the relative position of the attributes. Again, because grade is necessarily identified by both STUDENT and COURSE, it cannot reside with either entity by itself. An attribute like grade is called a "relationship attribute" or "intersection attribute."

An intersection attribute may arise first as a multi-valued attribute on some entity during the design process, only later to be questioned: "Why is this attribute here when it requires another entity to identify it?" When it is recognized that the attribute has to be identified by more than one entity, the attribute is moved to the relationship between the two (or more) entities that identify it.

Relationship attributes may occur with an ER diagram containing any cardinality, but one will most often find relationship attributes in the binary M:N situation. We now need to revisit our methodology to add a guideline for the attributes of a relationship:

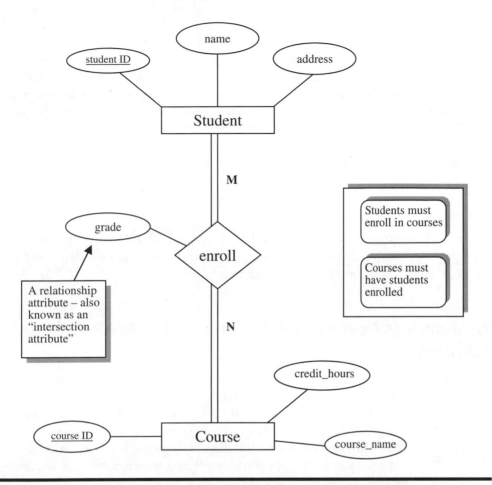

Figure 6.1   An ER Diagram of an M:N Relation with an Attribute of a Relationship

Step 6: State the exact nature of the relationships in structured English from all sides. For example, if a relationship is A:B::1:M, then there is a relationship from A to B, 1 to Many, and from B back to A, Many to 1.

And we add:

Step 6a: Examine the list of attributes and determine whether any of them need to be identified by two (or more) entities. If so, place the attribute on an appropriate relationship that joins the two entities.

Note that step 6a can also help in deciding which entities need to be related. If it had not been recognized up to this point that a relationship was needed, then the discovery of a relationship attribute would be a clear signal that such a relationship would be in order.

The grammar to describe the attribute of a relationship would be as follows:

The Attributes

> For atomic attributes, att(j): ...   [same as in previous chapters]
> For composite attributes, att(j): ...   [same as in previous chapters]
> For multivalued attributes, att(j): ...   [same as in previous chapters]
> For attributes of relationships att(j): ... [same as in previous chapters]

For the relationship between *Entity1* and *Entity2,* we will record a(n) att(j). The att(j) depends on both entities *Entity1* and *Entity2* for identification.

Example:

For the relationship between the STUDENT entity and the COURSE entity, we will record a grade attribute. The grade attribute depends on both the STUDENT and COURSE entities for identification.

Relationships Developing into Entities: The M:N Relationship Revisited

We previously defined the M:N relationship, and noted in the beginning of the chapter that an attribute often appears that should be associated with the relationship and not with one entity. The example was the attribute, grade, which would clearly not fit with either the STUDENT entity or the COURSE entity. In a sense, it appears that the relationship has itself taken on an entity quality. This observation is true because we have information (an attribute) that clearly belongs to the relationship.

There are two options in depicting this relationship-attribute situation. One option is to leave the attribute where it is, as we have shown it, on the relationship. If the number of attributes is small (one or two), then the sense of the diagram is still intact and the grammar representing the diagram will be understandable to the user.

The other option for relationship attributes would be to make the relationship an entity and tie both of the "identifying entities" to it. This option is shown in Figure 6.2. In this figure, the middle entity, STUDENT+COURSE, is depicted as weak because it depends entirely on the entities STUDENT and COURSE. Note that the participations are always full between the new, weak "intersection entity" and the relationships. Why? Because the weak entity must have a corresponding strong entity or it would not be there. The participation on the strong-relationship side (like between STUDENT and Rel1, or between COURSE and Rel2) can be partial or full, depending on whether it was partial or full originally. What would a partial COURSE–Rel2 connection mean? It would indicate that classes existed in the database that were not offered, and hence had no students in them.

Now that we have a STUDENT+COURSE entity (an intersecting entity), our grammatical description of this intersecting entity would be:

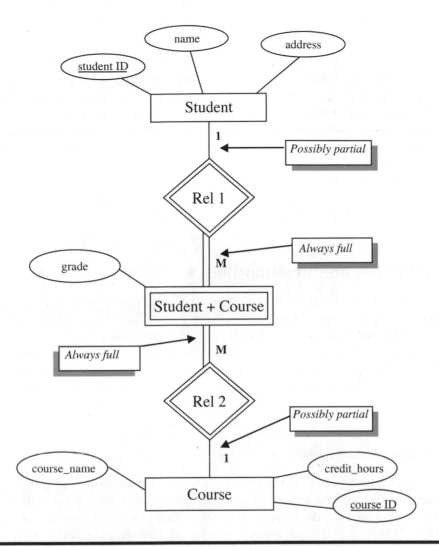

Figure 6.2   An ER Diagram of an M:N Relationship that Has Been Replaced with Two 1:M Relationships

The Entity

This database records data about STUDENT–COURSE combinations — STUDENT+COURSE. For each STUDENT+COURSE in the database, we record a grade.

The Attributes

For each STUDENT+COURSE, there always will be one and only one grade for each STUDENT+COURSE combination. The value for grade will not be subdivided.

The Keys

(d) No candidate keys (intersecting entity):
The STUDENT+COURSE entity does not have a candidate key of its own, but rather, each STUDENT+COURSE entity will be identified by keys belonging to the STUDENT and COURSE entities.

The latter statement is very close (and for a user, hopefully indistinguishable) from the key statements found in the "attribute on a relationship" grammar above:

For the relationship between STUDENT and COURSE, we will record a grade. The grade depends on both entities, STUDENT and COURSE, for identification.

More Entities and Relationships

In the handling of a database, we have to model the information presented. We will likely have situations that call for more than two entities and more than one binary relationship. Again, a binary relationship is a relationship between two entities. (Chapter 7 looks at ternary and higher relationship combinations.) This section deals with situations where the information about the database indicates that we have to expand our diagrams with more entities, but all the connections will be binary.

More than Two Entities

Let us again reconsider the STUDENT–COURSE ER diagram, Figure 6.1. If this database were oriented toward a college, the courses would have instructors and the instructors would be related to the courses. We would consider adding INSTRUCTOR to our database per our methodology steps 4 and 5, which say:

Step 4: If another entity is appropriate, draw the second entity with its attributes. Repeat step 2 to see if this entity should be further split into more entities.

Step 5: Connect entities with relationships (one or more) if relationships exist.

If we added instructors to the ER diagram, Figure 6.1, we might see something like Figure 6.3 (attributes other than the primary keys are intentionally left off to unclutter the diagram). The relationship between INSTRUCTOR and COURSE is teach — instructors teach many courses, a course is taught by an instructor (loosely speaking). The participation would be determined by the situation, but we will choose one for our example. Stated more precisely, we would say:

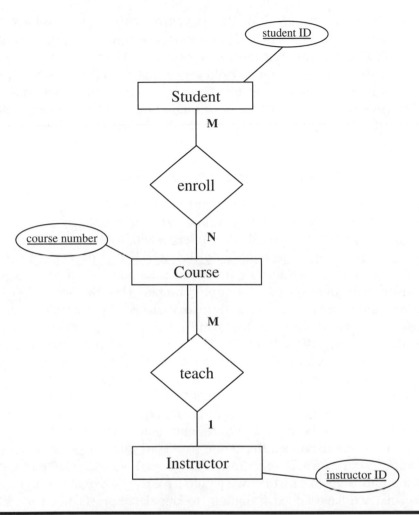

Figure 6.3   An ER Diagram (with Only Primary Keys) Showing a STUDENT/ COURSE/INSTRUCTOR Database

Pattern 4 — x:y::1:M, from the 1 Side, Partial Participation

Short: An instructor may teach many courses
which actually means:
Long: An instructor, but not necessarily all instructors, (which are recorded in the database) may teach many (one or more) courses. Some instructors may not teach courses.

Pattern 1 — x:y::M:1, from the M Side, Full Participation

Short: Courses must be taught by instructors.
which actually means:
Long: Courses, which are recorded in the database, must be taught by one and only one instructor. No course is taught by more than one instructor.

In this diagram (Figure 6.3), the INSTRUCTOR entity is related to the COURSE entity. There could be a relationship between the INSTRUCTOR entity and the STUDENT entity, but the relationships in Figure 6.3 are assumed to be the only ones that exist. One could argue that the other possible relationships are advisor, mentor, counselor, coach, ..., but remember that we are modeling only what exists and not what might be. We assume that the diagram represents the information given and only the information given.

Adding More Attributes that Evolve into Entities

As we have seen, ER diagrams evolve during the design/redesign process. One way ER diagrams evolve is to add attributes to various entities. Some attributes are going to be simple, functionally dependent additions. Functional dependency means that something is identifiable by that which it is dependent upon. For example, a social security number functionally identifies a name, and name is functionally dependent on social security number. This functional dependency means that anywhere a certain value for social security number exists in the database, you can be sure that the same name will appear with it. Consider adding the attribute instructor name. The addition enhances the diagram and instructor name is functionally dependent on the attribute, instructor ID.

Now consider adding "building" to each of the entities. Students live in buildings (dorms), courses are taught in buildings (classrooms and labs), instructors have offices in buildings. "Building" can be added as an attribute of each of the three entities and not be considered an entity unto itself. Why? Because at this stage, we have not expressed the desire to record information about buildings. If buildings (dorm rooms, class rooms, office rooms) were considered as attribute items for appropriate entities, then we would have the ER diagram as in Figure 6.4.

Now that we have added "building" to our database (Figure 6.4), suppose we evolve yet again to where we now decide that we do want to record more information about buildings; or put another way, we want to make BUILDING an entity. We would then have to connect other entities to BUILDING with appropriate relationships. Such a design is depicted in Figure 6.5. Whether we begin with the idea of BUILDING as an entity or evolve to it by starting with STUDENTS, COURSES, and INSTRUCTORS, we need to be constantly asking the question, "Is this item in the ER diagram one that we want to record information about, or not? Should this be an entity?" In Figure 6.5, we have depicted BUILDING as an entity and hence we will want to add attributes to it. For an embellished ER diagram with more attributes and cardinalities, see Figure 6.6.

Checkpoint 6.1

1. In Figure 6.6, why is BUILDING an entity and not an attribute of another entity?
2. In Figure 6.6, why is the room number attribute attached to the *lives in* relationship rather than the STUDENT entity?

3. What will make you decide whether an attribute should be connected to ENTITYA or ENTITYB or, on the relationship connecting ENTITYA and ENTITYB?
4. Why are all the lines leaving BUILDING (on Figure 6.6) single lines (partial participation)?
5. According Figure 6.6, does a student have to enroll in a course?
6. According to Figure 6.6, how many courses can an instructor teach?

More Evolution of the Database

Let us reconsider the ER diagram in Figure 6.6. As the diagram is analyzed, the user might ask, "Why is a room number attribute not included for the

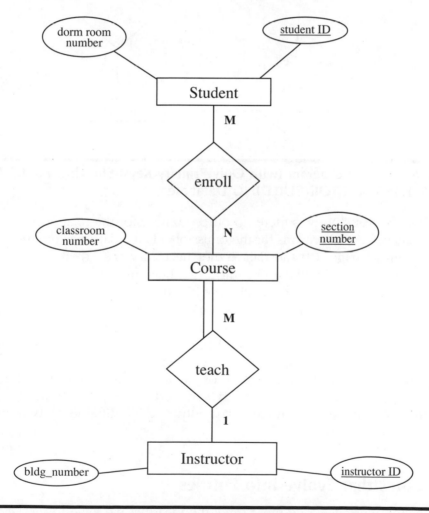

Figure 6.4   An ER Diagram (with Only Primary Keys) Showing a STUDENT/ COURSE/INSTRUCTOR Database with "Building" as an Attribute

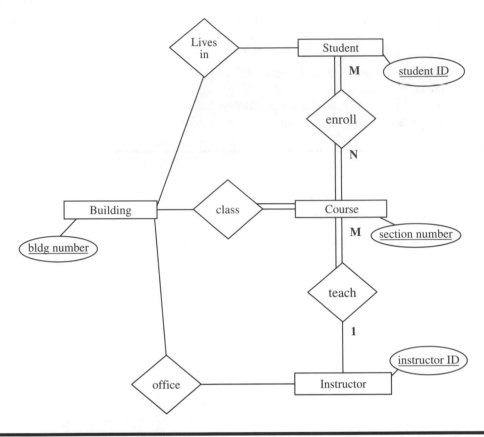

Figure 6.5   An ER Diagram (with Only Primary Keys) Showing a STUDENT/ COURSE/INSTRUCTOR/BUILDING Database

relationship, class?" Why is there no office number for the relationship, office? There may be several reasons for the omission: (1) the data was not mentioned in the analysis stage; (2) the data is not necessary (i.e., there may be only one classroom per building or office numbers may not be recorded for advisors); or (3) it was an oversight and the data should be added. Suppose now we decide that room number is important for all of the relationships or entities. Suppose that we want to identify the room number associated with instructors and buildings, courses and buildings, and students and buildings. We might "evolve" the diagram to that of Figure 6.7.

In this case, we have information attached to BUILDING: building occupancy, the maintenance supervisor, and the square footage of the building. We have room number as an attribute identifiable by two entities in each case.

Attributes that Evolve into Entities

This section illustrates, one more time, the idea that we have to model "what is" and not necessarily "what might be." Also, we again see how an attribute might become an entity. Consider, for example, the following data that will

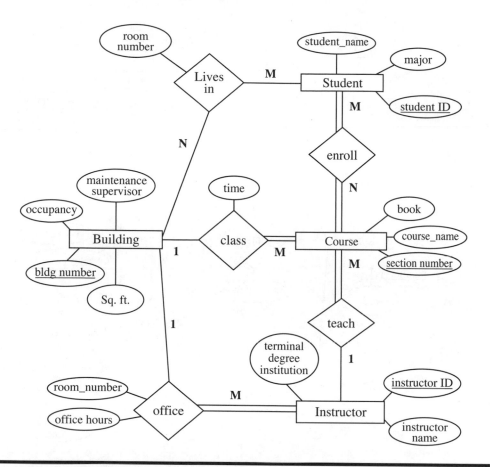

Figure 6.6   An ER Diagram Showing a STUDENT/COURSE/INSTRUCTOR/ BUILDING Database

go into an ER diagram/database: a course name, course number, credits, instructor name, and book. Example:

```
'Database','COP 4710',3,'Earp','Elmasri/Navathe'
```

The beginning ER diagram might look like Figure 6.8, "An ER Diagram of the COURSE entity in a database." Why "might look like..."? The answer lies in eliciting correct requirements from our user.

  If all of the information that was ever to be recorded about this data was mentioned above, then this single entity ER diagram would describe the database. However, one could realistically argue that things that we have described as attributes could themselves be entities. Both the instructor and the book would be candidates for being diagrammed as entities if the envisioned database called for it.

  Consider a scenario in which one might choose to expand or redesign the database to include information about instructors. If this were the case, we might want to go beyond recording the instructor name and also include such attributes as the instructor's department, date_hired, and the school where the

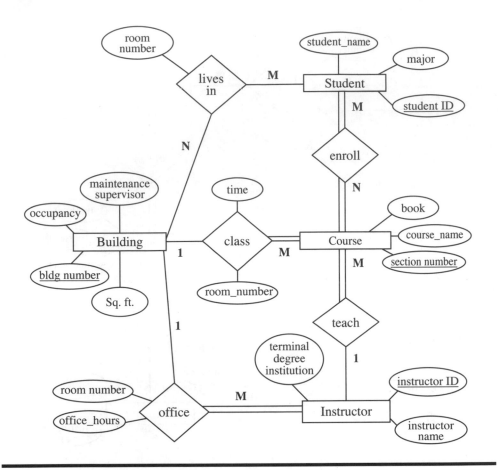

Figure 6.7   An ER Diagram Showing a STUDENT/COURSE/INSTRUCTOR/ BUILDING Database with the "room number" for the Three Relations

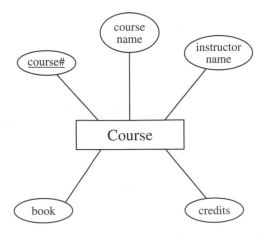

Figure 6.8   An ER Diagram with COURSE Entity in a Database

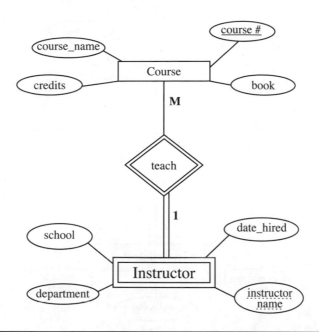

Figure 6.9   An ER Diagram of the COURSE–INSTRUCTOR Database

instructor received the terminal degree. With the additional information about INSTRUCTORS, the ER diagram would have two entities and would look like Figure 6.9.

In Figure 6.9, we have depicted the INSTRUCTOR entity as weak because of the presumed non-uniqueness of instructor names and the dependence on COURSE. If the instructor were identified uniquely with an attribute like instructor social security number, and if instructors could exist independent of course, then the entity could become strong and would look like Figure 6.10. The idea of this section, then, is to bring out the point that an entity is not an entity just because one might want to record information "someday." There would have to be some planned intent to include the data that would be identified by the entity. Further, the definition of weak or strong entity would depend on the identifying information that was to be provided.

Finally, if no information about instructors were ever planned, then the first ER diagram (Figure 6.10) would well describe the database. We will leave as an exercise the extension of Figure 6.10 to include BOOK as an entity.

Recursive Relationships

A recursive relationship is where the same entity participates more than once in different roles. Recursive relationships are also sometimes called ***unary*** relationships.

Consider, for example, the idea of personnel relations in a company. Personnel are likely to have an employee number, a name, etc. In addition to existing as an entity for all employees of an organization, there are relationships between individuals of the entity set, PERSONNEL. The most

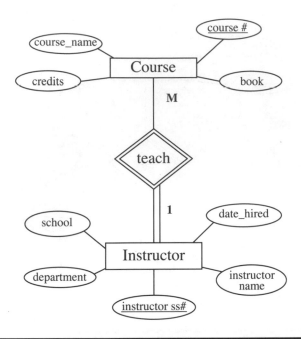

Figure 6.10   An ER Diagram of the COURSE–INSTRUCTOR Database

obvious relationship is that of employee–supervisor or personnel–supervisor. How would we depict the personnel–supervisor relationship when we have only one entity? The answer is shown in Figure 6.11.

Figure 6.11 shows the entity, PERSONNEL, with some simple attributes. Then, the relationship of supervise is added and connected to PERSONNEL

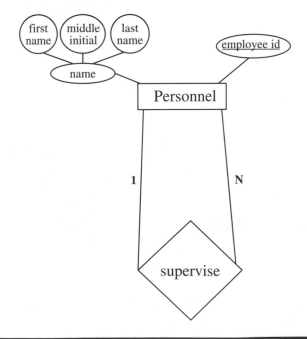

Figure 6.11   A Classic Recursive Relationship PERSONNEL–SUPERVISOR

on both ends. The cardinality of the relationship is 1:N, which means that one employee (personnel) can supervise many other employees but can only be supervised by one employee. We use partial participation from the supervisor side because not all personnel are supervisors — an employee *may* supervise many employees. The participation of the supervised employee is also partial. Although most employees are supervised by some, one supervisor, some employee will be at the top of the hierarchy with no supervisor. In recursive relationships, we are representing a hierarchy. All hierarchies have a top spot with no "supervision." All hierarchies are always partial–partial.

So, when there arises a relationship between individuals within the same entity set, it would be improper to have two entities because most of the information in the entities is basically the same. If we created two entities, then we would have redundancy in the database. Using the above example, if we used two different entities rather than a recursive relationship, then an employee would be recorded in two different entities.

Recursive Relationships and Structural Constraints

Recursive relationships can only have partial participation in relationships, but the cardinality can be one-to-one, one-to-many, or many-to-many. Full participation in a recursive relationship would mean that every instance of an entity participates in a relationship with itself, which would not make sense.

Next we look at some examples of cardinalities as interpreted in recursive relationships.

One-to-One Recursive Relationship (Partial Participation on Both Sides)

Figure 6A show us an example of an entity, PERSONNEL, that is related to itself through a married to relationship. This means that a person in this database can be married to one other person in this same database.

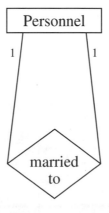

Figure 6A   One-to-One Recursive Relationship (Partial Participation on Both Sides)

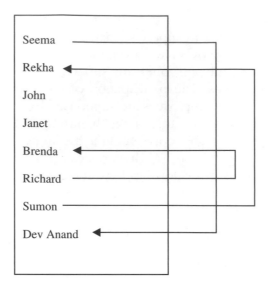

Figure 6B   Instances of One-to-One Recursive Relationship (Partial Participation on Both Sides)

Some instances of this relationship are shown in Figure 6B. From Figure 6B we can see that Seema is married to Dev Anand, Sumon is married to Rekha, etc.

One-to-Many Recursive Relationship (Partial Participation on Both Sides)

This is the most common recursive relationship. An example of this relationship may be where one employee may supervise many other employees (as shown in Figure 6C). As mentioned before, this is a hierarchical relationship and is always partial–partial.

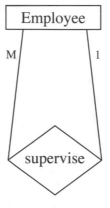

Figure 6C   One-to-Many Recursive Relationship (Partial Participation on Both Sides)

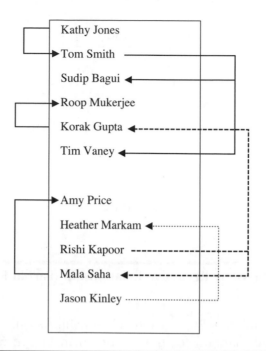

Figure 6D   Instances of One-to-Many Recursive Relationship (Partial Participation on Both Sides)

Instances of this relationship are shown in Figure 6D. From Figure 6D we can see that Tom Smith supervises Sudip Bagui and Tim Vaney, Rishi Kapoor supervises Mala Sinha and Korak Gupta, Korak Gupta supervises Roop Mukerjee, etc.

Many-to-Many Recursive Relationship (Partial on Both Sides)

In this example we could say that courses may be prerequisities for zero or more other courses. This relationship is depicted in Figure 6E. The sense of prerequisite here is not hierarchical, but more like a situation where there are many courses that are interrelated.

Multiple Relationships

Thus far we mostly discussed that two entities can have a (one) relationship. This section discusses how two entities can have more than one relationship (but the relationships here are still binary relationships).

Consider a diagram that has two entities: STUDENT and FACULTY. Suppose we have no other entities in the database. Suppose further that the STUDENT entity has the following attributes: name, student #, birthdate, and the name of the high school (high_school) from which the student graduated. The FACULTY entity could have the following attributes: name, social security number (SS#), department affiliation, office_number. Now consider two relationships: *instructor* and *advisor*. There are only two entities here and

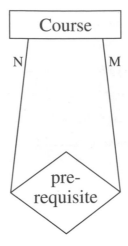

Figure 6E   Many-to-Many Recursive Relationship (Partial Participation on Both Sides)

yet there are two relationships. Each relationship should be given its own "diamond." The ER diagram for this is shown in Figure 6.12

In this diagram, all relationships are arbitrarily shown as partial; that is, there will be some faculty who do not advise students, and some students who are not instructed by faculty. In constructing ER diagrams, one has to include however many relationships exist. It would be incorrect to try to make a relationship do "double duty" and stand for two different relationship ideas.

In this example, an embellishment might include intersection data for the instruct relationship (a grade in a course, for example). Intersection data for the advise relationship could be date_assigned, time of last_meeting, etc. as shown in Figure 6.12A.

The placing of relationships in the ER diagram is covered in our ER design methodology in step 5, which we will redefine here:

The original step 5 was:

Step 5: Connect entities with relationships if relationships exist.

We can add to this guideline that if multiple relationships are present, they are added to the diagram; however, this is likely redundant, so we will simply append the phrase "(one or more)":

Step 5: Connect entities with relationships (one or more) if relationships exist.

The Derived or Redundant Relationship

Many authors describe a redundant (Martin, 1983) or derived (Hawryszkiew-ycz, 1984) relationship that could arise in a relationship "loop" like that of

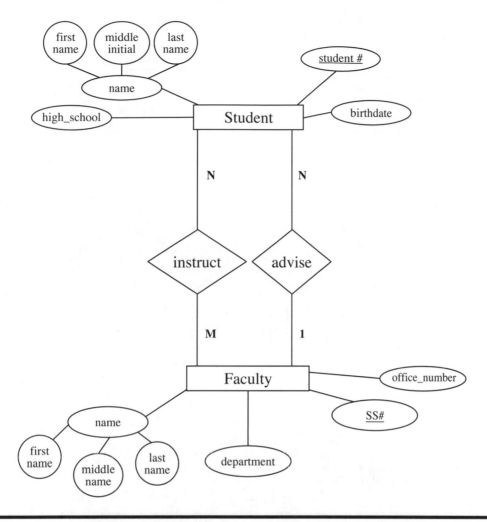

Figure 6.12   An ER Diagram with Two Entities and Two Relationships

Figure 6.13. The loop notion comes from the pictorial idea that the lines form a closed graph (which is actually more like a rectangle, but we are going to call it a loop). The idea of redundancy is that because students take courses and each course is taught by an instructor, you do not need a *taught by* relationship because you can get that information without the extra relationship. If such a relationship exists, then it should be excised, but there are caveats.

First, one has to be sure that the redundant relationship is truly redundant. If the added relation were advised by instead of taught by, then the relationship should stay because it has a completely different sense than taught by.

Second, if the relationship loop is present, it may mean that only one of the two redundant relationships should be kept and the semantics should point to which one. In Figure 6.13, the INSTRUCTOR is more likely related to a COURSE than to a STUDENT. So, the better choice of which relationship to keep would be the original one: teach. It is very conceivable that a designer might have included the taught by relationship first, only later to include the

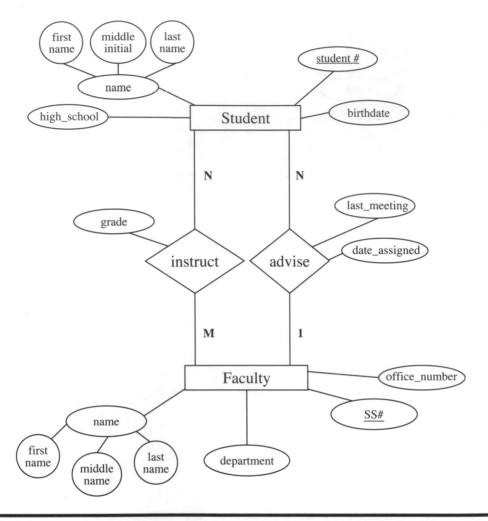

Figure 6.12A   An ER Diagram with Two Entities and Two Relationships and Some Intersection Attributes

teach relationship. Then, by examining the diagram for loops, one can deduce that the taught by was redundant.

Third, one or both of the relationships may have an intersection attribute that would suggest which relationship (or both) should be kept. In Figure 6.14, we included the attribute, time, which was put with the teach relationship as an instructor teaches a course at some time.

The idea of derived or redundant relationships causes us to suggest one more step in our methodology:

Step 6b.
Examine the diagram for loops that might indicate redundant relationships. If a relationship is truly redundant, excise the redundant relationship.

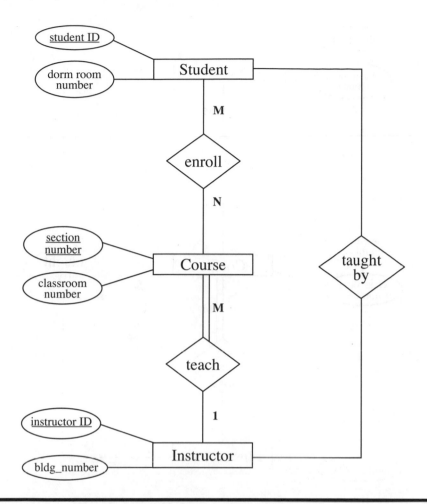

Figure 6.13 An ER Diagram Showing a STUDENT/COURSE/INSTRUCTOR Database with a "Redundant" Relationship

Checkpoint 6.2

1. What is a recursive relationship?
2. What would you look for if you are trying to see if a relationship is recursive?
3. What kinds of structural constraints can recursive relationships have?
4. Can recursive relationships have full participation? Why or why not?
5. How is the recursive relationship denoted diagrammatically in the Chen-like ER model?
6. Can the same two entities have more than one relationship?
7. How would you determine if a relationship is redundant?

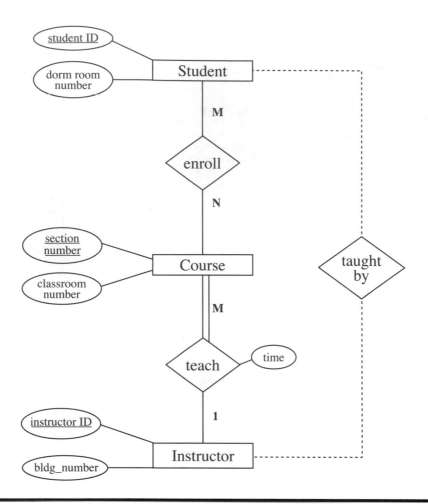

Figure 6.14 An ER Diagram Showing a STUDENT/COURSE/INSTRUCTOR Database with a "Redundant" Relationship

Optional Section

We call the next section, entitled "An Alternative ER Notation for Specifying Structural Constraints on Relationships," an optional section because it is not really necessary to know or use this section to fully understand the ER design methodology or to arrive at a good database product. However, some may find this section more descriptive.

An Alternative ER Notation for Specifying Structural Constraints on Relationships

Thus far we have discussed cardinality ratios in terms of their upper bounds (the maximum cardinality), shown by the "M" or "N" in the ER diagrams (shown in this and previous chapters). You will recall (from Chapter 4) that

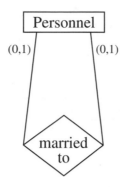

Figure 6.15   Recursive Relationship with (min, max) Ratios

cardinality is a rough measure of the number of entity instances in one entity set that can be related to instances in another entity set.

This section describes an alternative ER notation for specifying structural constraints on relationships. This notation will associate a pair of numbers (*min, max*) with each participation of an instance of an entity in an instance of a relationship. This *min* and *max* can provide more information about the entities and the relationships.

The *min* is the minimum number of instances in one entity set that can be related to an instance of a relationship. The *min* can be between zero and the maximum. If the *min* is zero, it implies that every instance of an entity does not have to participate in an instance of the relationship. This, in effect, means partial participation. If the *min* is greater than zero, this implies full participation. We now present an ER diagram with (*min, max*) ratios.

First, let us start with the recursive relationship shown in Figure 6.15. The (*min, max*) of (0,1) means that each personnel may or may not be married (shown by the zero for the min), and can only be married to at most one personnel (shown by the max). Next, look at Figure 6.16. From this figure we can say that a student may not be advised by any faculty, and may be advised by up to two faculty members (shown by the minimum of zero, and maximum of two [i.e., (0,2)]). A faculty member can advise between zero (0) and 30 students. A faculty member can instruct between zero (0) and 40 students. And, a student must be instructed by one faculty member, and can be instructed by up to two (2) faculty members.

Checkpoint 6.3 (Optional)

1. What lower bound of cardinality does full participation imply?
2. What does a min/max ratio of (1,1) between two entities imply?
3. What kind of participation ratio (full participation or partial participation) does a min/max ratio of (0,1) imply?

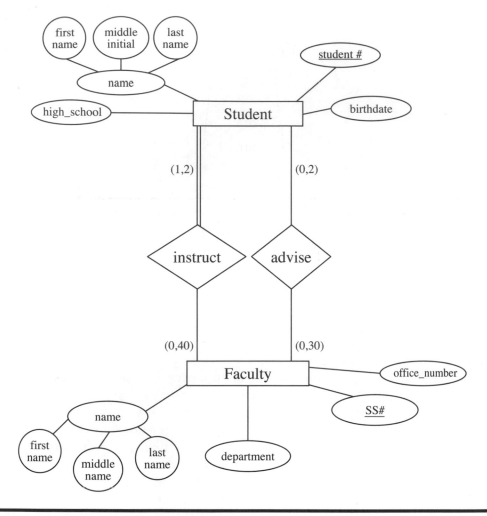

Figure 6.16   An ER Diagram Showing an Alternative ER Notation for Specifying Structural Constraints

Review of the Methodology

To review, our methodology for designing ER diagrams has now evolved to the following:

ER Design Methodology

Step 1: Select one, primary entity from the database requirements-description and show attributes to be recorded for that entity. Label keys if appropriate and show some sample data.

Step 2: Use structured English for entities, attributes, and keys to describe the database that has been elicited.

Step 3: Examine attributes in the existing entities (possibly with user assistance) to find out if information about one of the entities is to be recorded. (Note: We change "primary" to "existing" because we redo step 3 as we add new entities.)

Step 3a: If information about an attribute is needed, then make the attribute an entity, and then

Step 3b: Define the relationship back to the original entity.

Step 4: If another entity is appropriate, draw the second entity with its attributes. Repeat steps 2 and 3 to see if this entity should be further split into more entities.

Step 5: Connect entities with relationships (one or more) if relationships exist.

Step 6: State the exact nature of the relationships in structured English from all sides. For example, if a relationship is A:B::1:M, then there is a relationship from A(1) to B(M) and from B(M) back to A(1).

Step 6a: Examine the list of attributes and determine whether any of them need to be identified by two (or more) entities. If so, place the attribute on an appropriate relationship that joins the two entities.

Step 6b: Examine the diagram for loops, which might indicate redundant relationships. If a relationship is truly redundant, excise the redundant relationship.

Step 7: Show some sample data.

Step 8: Present the "as designed" database to the user, complete with the English for entities, attributes, keys, and relationships. Refine the diagram as necessary.

The grammar to describe our entities, attributes and keys has evolved to this:

The Entity: This database records data about ENTITY. For each ENTITY in the database, we record att(1), att(2), att(3), ... att(n).

The Attributes:

For atomic attributes, att(j):

For each ENTITY, there always will be one and only one att(j) for each ENTITY. The value for att(j) will not be subdivided.

For composite attributes, att(j):

For each ENTITY, we will record att(j), which is composed of x, y, z, ... (x, y, z) are the component parts of att(j).

For multi-valued attributes, att(j):

For each ENTITY, we will record att(j)s. There may be more than one att(j) recorded for each ENTITY.

For attributes of relationships att(j):

For the relationship between ENTITY1 and ENTITY2 we will record a(n) att(j). The att(j) depends on both entities, ENTITY1 and ENTITY2, for identification.

The Keys:

More than one candidate key (strong entity):

For each ENTITY, we will have the following candidate keys: att(j), att(k), ... (where j, k are candidate key attributes)

One candidate key (strong entity):

For each ENTITY, we will have the following primary key: att(j)

No candidate keys (perhaps a weak entity):

For each ENTITY, we do not assume that any attribute will be unique enough to identify individual entities.

No candidate keys (perhaps an intersecting entity):

For each ENTITY, we do not assume that any attribute will be unique enough to identify individual entities.

Mapping Rules for Recursive Relationships

Recursive relationships are binary 1:1, 1:N, or M:N relationships. We discussed the mapping rules for these types of relationships in Chapter 4. In that chapter, the mapping rule was discussed for two entities. If there is only one entity, the rules basically stay the same; but rather than including the primary key of one entity (ENTITY_A) in another entity (ENTITY_B), the primary key of ENTITY_A is reincluded in ENTITY_A.

M5 — For recursive entities — two types of mapping rules can be developed:

M5a — For 1:N recursive relationships — reinclude the primary key of the table with the recursive relationship in the same table, giving it some other name.

For example, Figure 6.11 will get mapped to something like:

		PERSONNEL		
name.first	*name.last*	*name.mi*	*employee_id*	*super_id*
Richard	Earp	W	8945	9090
Boris	Yelsen		9090	null
Helga	Hogan	H	3841	9090
Sudip	Bagui	K	8767	9090
Tina	Tanner		5050	8945

M5b — For M:N recursive relationships, create a separate table for the relationship (as in mapping rule M3a).

As an example, if we assumed that Figure 6.11 was an M:N relationship, then Figure 6.11 would map to the above table (PERSONNEL) and:

PERSONNEL_SUPERVISOR	
employee_id	*super_id*
8945	9090
9090	null
3841	9090
8767	9090
5050	8945

Checkpoint 6.4

1. Map the recursive relationship shown in Figure 6C to a relational database and show some sample data.
2. If Figure 6C was an M:N relationship, how would you map this recursive relationship to a relational database? Show the mapping with some sample data.

Chapter Summary

This chapter viewed the different aspects of binary relationships in ER diagrams and refined several of the steps in the ER design methodology. The refining of the ER design methodology means a continuous assessment and reassessment of the ER diagram that is drawn after discussion with the users. The idea that relationships could have attributes, how attributes evolve into entities, recursive relationships, and derived and redundant relationships were discussed with examples and diagrams. The ER design methodology steps were refined to include all of the above into the new and evolving methodology.

Toward the end of the chapter, an alternative ER notation for specifying structural constraints on relationships was presented. Upon completing this chapter, the reader or database creator should be able to efficiently design a database with binary relationships. Chapter 7 deals with ternary and other higher-order relationships.

Chapter 6 Exercises

In each of the exercises that follow, the admonition to "construct an ER diagram" implies not only the diagram, but also the structured grammatical description of the diagram.

Exercise 6.1

Define and state in precise terms the cardinality and participation in Figure 6.5, the STUDENT/COURSE/INSTRUCTOR/BUILDING database. Discuss the structural constraints of Figure 6.5. Under what circumstances would the structural constraints depicted be correct or incorrect?

Exercise 6.2

Consider the following data and construct an ER diagram — use structured grammar to rationalize your constraints. The data: horse name, race, owner, odds at post, post position, date of race, order of finish, year to date earnings, owner name and address.

Exercise 6.3

In this chapter we described a database that had two entities: COURSE and INSTRUCTOR (refer to Figure 6.10). Book was left as an attribute of COURSE. Extend the database to include BOOK as an entity. Attributes of BOOK might include: book title, author, price, edition, publisher.

Exercise 6.4

Refer to Figure 6.7. Change Figure 6.7 to include the following information: One building can have a maximum of 99 students living in it. A student has to enroll in at least one class, and can enroll in a maximum of five classes. A class has to enroll at least five students, and can enroll a maximum of 35 students. A instructor may or may not teach a class, and can teach up to three classes. A course has to have one instructor teaching it, and only one instructor can teach a particular course. An instructor may or may not have an office, and can have up to two offices. A building may or may not have an office, and can have up to 15 offices. A course has to be offered in one classroom, and can only be offered in one classroom.

References

Bracchi, G., Paolini, P., and Pelagatti, G., "Binary Logical Associations in Data Modelling," *Modelling in Data Base Management Systems,* G.M. Nijssen, Ed., North-Holland, Amsterdam, 1976.

Earp, R. and Bagui, S., "Binary Relationships in Entity Relationships in Entity Relationship (ER) Diagrams," *Data Base Management,* Auerbach Publications, Boca Raton, FL, 22-10-43, 1–17, April 2000.

Hawryszkiewycz, I., *Database Analysis and Design*, SRA, Chicago, 1984.

Mark, L., "Defining Views in the Binary Relationship Model," *Information System,* 12, 3 (1987), p. 281–294.

Martin, J., *Managing the Data-Base Environment*, Prentice Hall, Englewood Cliffs, NJ, 1983.

Sanders, L., *Data Modeling*, Boyd & Fraser Publishing, Danvers, MA, 1995.

Teorey, T.J., *Database Modeling and Design*, Morgan Kaufman, San Francisco, 1999.

Case Study:
West Florida Mall (continued)

Thus far in our case study, we have developed the major entities and relationships and mapped these to a relational database (with some sample data). Then, upon reviewing step 7, which says:

Step 7: Present the "as-designed" database to the user, complete with the English for entities, attributes, keys, and relationships. Refine the diagram as necessary.

Suppose we got some additional input from the user:

> An employee can also be a department manager, and a department manager can manage at most one department. We have to store information on the department manager — the name, social security number, which store he/she is working for, which department he/she is working for. A department manager supervises at least one employee, and may manage several employees.

Upon reviewing these additional specifications, we can see that we have a recursive relationship developing here, because an employee can be a department manager supervising other employees.

So, using mapping rule M5a, we will reinclude the primary key of the EMPLOYEE entity in itself, giving us the following EMPLOYEE relation:

EMPLOYEE				
ename	essn	dnum	snum	dm_ssn
Kaitlyn	987–754–9865	501	1	276–263–9182
Fred	276–263–9182	502	1	null
Katie	982–928–2726	503	1	987–754–9865
Seema	837–937–9373	501	1	276–263–9182
.				
.				
.				

This recursive relationship is also shown in Figure 6.17.

So, in summary, our relational database has now developed to (without the data):

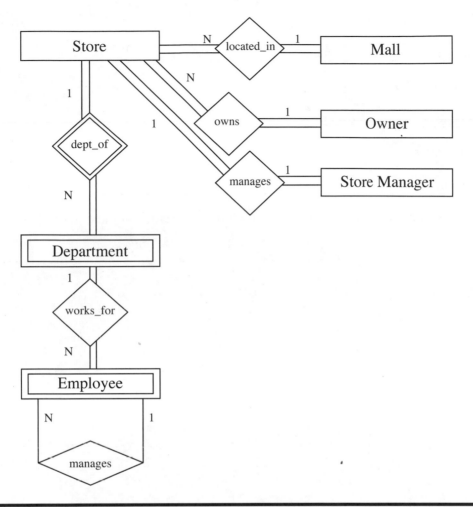

Figure 6.17   An ER Diagram of West Florida Mall Developed Thus Far

MALL-Store

name	store_name

MALL

name	address

STORE

sloc	sname	snum	mall_name	so_owner	sm_ssn

OWNER

so_ssn	so_name	so_off_phone	so_address

STORE MANAGER

sm_ssn	sm_name	salary

DEPARTMENT

dname	dnum	snum

EMPLOYEE

ename	essn	dnum	snum	dm_ssn

We will continue with the development of this case study at the end of Chapter 8.

Chapter 7

Ternary and Higher-Order ER Diagrams

Chapter Topics

Binary or Ternary Relationship?
Structural Constraints for Ternary Relationships
  Many-to-Many-to-Many (M:M:M) Structural Constraint
  Example of *n*-ary Relationship
  n-ary Relations Do Not Preclude Binary Relations
  Methodology and Grammar for the *n*-ary Relationship
  The More Exact Grammar
  Grammar in a Partial Participation, Ternary Relationship with a 1-Relationship
Ternary Relationships from Relationship–Relationship Situations
n-ary Relationships that May Be Resolved into Binary Relationships
Mapping Ternary Diagrams to a Relational Database
Chapter Summary
Chapter 7 Exercises
References

All relationships that we have dealt with thus far in previous chapters have been binary relationships. Although binary relationships seem natural to most of us, in reality it is sometimes necessary to connect three or more entities. If a relationship connects three entities, it is called ternary or "3-ary." If a relationship connects three or more entities (*n* entities), it is called an "*n*-ary" relationship, where *n* equals the number of entities that participate in the relationship. *n*-ary relationships are also referred to as "higher-order" relationships.

In this chapter we consider relationships that connect three or more entities. First we look at ternary (3-ary) relationships. Ternary relationships arise for

165

three main reasons: (1) if we have intersection attributes that require three different entities to identify the attribute, (2) if we have a relationship of a relationship, and (3) by reverse-engineering. Because we discuss reverse-engineering in Chapter 9, we will not discuss the development of ternary relationships from reverse-engineering in this chapter.

In this chapter we first discuss how intersection attributes create ternary relationships, and then look at the structural constraints of ternary relationships. Next, we discuss how ternary and other *n*-ary relationships do not preclude binary relationships, and how some ternary diagrams can be resolved into binary relationships. The development of ternary relationships from relationships of relationships is also discussed. Step 6 of the ER design methodology is also redefined in this chapter to include ternary and other higher-order relationships.

Binary or Ternary Relationship?

Ternary relationships are required when binary relationships are not sufficient to accurately describe the semantics of an association among three entities. In this section we explain the difference between a binary and a ternary relationship with the help of an example, and also show how an intersection attribute necessitates a ternary relationship.

In the binary case, we found that relationships existed between entities and that these relationships would have structural constraints (cardinality and participation). Further, we found that attributes of relationships were also possible. In particular, we found that the M:N relationship often spawned an attribute, which we called an intersection attribute (recall the STUDENT/ CLASS M:N relationship and the intersection attribute, grade, as shown in Figure 6.1). In the binary relationship case, we made the point that an attribute like grade would infer that an M:N binary relationship must exist. Whether one determined the M:N relationship first or found the "orphaned" attribute first would not matter; the end result would be an M:N relationship with an intersection attribute.

Cases exist in databases when a relationship between more than two entities is needed. The usual case would be to find one of these "orphaned" attributes that necessitated the *n*-ary relationship. Consider the following example.

You have a database for a company that contains the entities, PRODUCT, SUPPLIER, and CUSTOMER. The usual relationships might be PRODUCT/ SUPPLIER where the company buys products from a supplier — a normal binary relationship. The intersection attribute for PRODUCT/SUPPLIER is wholesale_price (as shown in Figure 7.1A). Now consider the CUSTOMER entity, and that the customer buys products. If all customers pay the same price for a product, regardless of supplier, then you have a simple binary relationship between CUSTOMER and PRODUCT. For the CUSTOMER/ PRODUCT relationship, the intersection attribute is retail_price (as shown in Figure 7.1B).

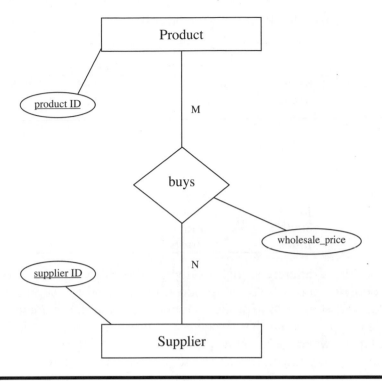

Figure 7.1A A Binary Relationship of PRODUCT and SUPPLIER and an Intersection Attribute, wholesale_price

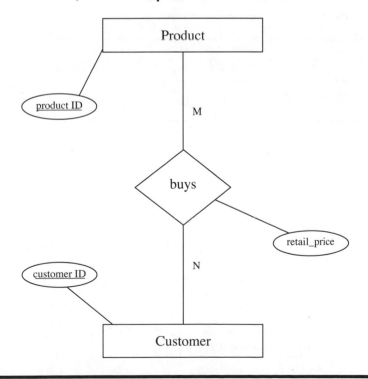

Figure 7.1B A Binary Relationship of PRODUCT and CUSTOMER and an Intersection Attribute, retail_price

Some sample data for Figure 7.1A would be:

PRODUCT–SUPPLIER		
productId	*supplierId*	*wholesale_price*
Beans	AcmeBean Co	1.49
Beans	Baker Bean Co.	1.57
Carrots	Joe's Carrots	0.89

Some sample data for Figure 7.1B would be:

PRODUCT–CUSTOMER		
customerID	*productId*	*retail_price*
Jones	Beans	2.67
Smith	Beans	2.67
Jones	Carrots	1.57

Now consider a different scenario. Suppose the customer buys products but the price depends not only on the product, but also on the supplier. Suppose you needed a customerID, a productID, and a supplierID to identify a price. Now you have an attribute that depends on three things and hence you have a relationship between three entities (a ternary relationship) that will have the intersection attribute, price. This situation is depicted in Figure 7.2.

Figure 7.2 represents the entities PRODUCT, SUPPLIER, and CUSTOMER, and a relationship, *buy*, among all three entities, shown by a single relationship diamond attached to all three entities.

Some sample data for Figure 7.2 would be:

PRODUCT–SUPPLIER–CUSTOMER			
customerID	*productID*	*supplierID*	*price*
Jones	Beans	Acme	2.65
Jones	Beans	Baker	2.77
Jones	Carrots	Joe's	1.57

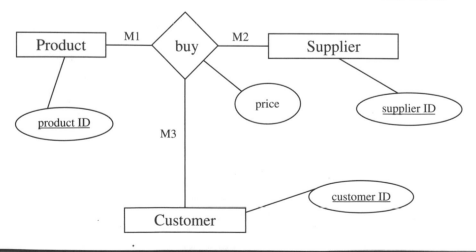

Figure 7.2   An ER Diagram (with Only Primary Keys) Showing a Three-Way Relationship

This ternary case is more realistic because customers generally pay different prices for the same product by different manufacturers or suppliers. For different suppliers, one might also assume different prices for a product at different points in time. Also, for customers, one might assume that some items are bought on sale, some not. Another intersection attribute (see Figure 7.2) could be date, which could be the date of the sale of a product to a customer by a supplier.

In the case of higher-order relationships, they are most often found by finding an attribute that necessitates the existence of the *n*-ary relationship. Next we look at the structural constraints of ternary relationships.

Structural Constraints for Ternary Relationships

Ternary relationships can have the following types of structural constraints: one-to-one-to-one (1:1:1), one-to-one-to-many (1:1:M), one-to-many-to-many (1:M:M), and many-to-many-many (M:M:M), with full or partial participation on each one of the sides. Below is an example of the (M:M:M) with partial participation on all sides:

Many-to-Many-to-Many (M:M:M) Structural Constraint

Figure 7A shows an example of a M:M:N relationship using three entities: PRODUCT, SUPPLIER, and CUSTOMER. This figure shows that many customers can buy many products from many suppliers, at different prices.

Instances of this relationship can be illustrated as shown in Figure 7B.

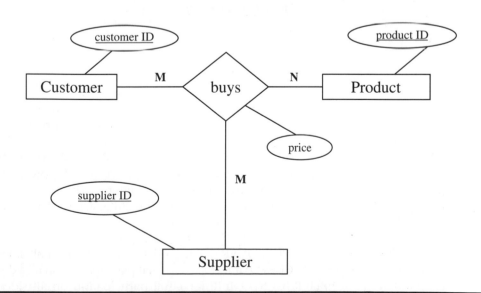

Figure 7A   An ER Diagram Showing a Ternary Many-to-Many-to-Many Relationship (Partial Participation on All Sides)

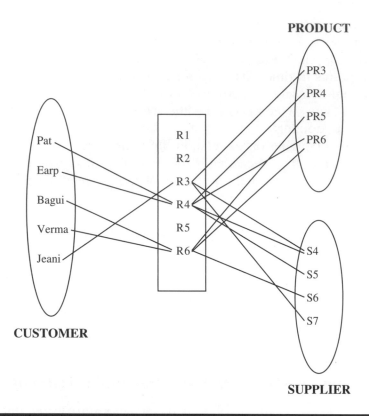

Figure 7B   Instances of a Ternary Many-to-Many-to-Many for CUSTOMER:PRODUCT:SUPPLIER Relationship

Checkpoint 7.1

1. What is a ternary relationship?
2. What is an *n*-ary relationship?
3. What are "higher order" relationships?
4. Using the three entities used above (PRODUCT, SUPPLIER, and CUSTOMER), draw an ER diagram that depicts the following: A customer must buy one and only one product from a supplier at a particular price on a particular date.
5. Using the three entities used above (PRODUCT, SUPPLIER, and CUSTOMER), draw an ER diagram that depicts the following: A supplier must supply many products to many customers at different prices on different dates.
6. Think of some more intersection attributes for the PRODUCT, SUPPLIER, and CUSTOMER ternary example given above.
7. What situations might create each of the following structural constraints?
   a. PRODUCT: SUPPLIER: CUSTOMER::1:1:1, partial participation on all sides.
   b. PRODUCT: SUPPLIER: CUSTOMER::1:M:M, partial participation on all sides.
   c. PRODUCT: SUPPLIER: CUSTOMER::1:1:1 full participation on all sides.

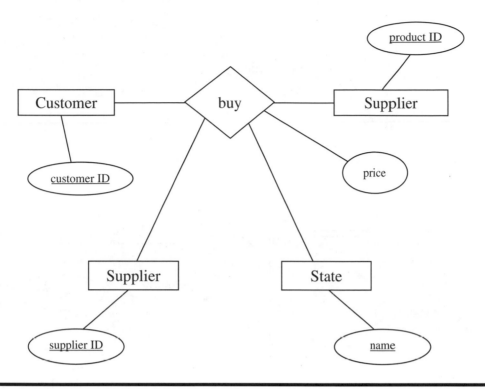

Figure 7.3   An ER Diagram Showing an *n*-ary Relationship

Example of *n*-ary Relationship

An *n*-ary relationship describes the association among *n* entities. For our ternary example, we said that the price was dependent on a PRODUCT, SUPPLIER, and CUSTOMER. If we now say that the price is dependent on a PRODUCT, SUPPLIER, CUSTOMER, as well as STATE, then we are saying that the attribute price is dependent on four entities, and hence an *n*-ary (in this case, a 4-ary) relationship. In an *n*-ary (or, in this case, 4-ary) relationship, a single relationship diamond connects the *n* (4) entities, as shown in Figure 7.3. Here, too, the intersection attribute is price. More attributes on the entities would be expected.

n-ary Relationships Do Not Preclude Binary Relationships

Just because there is a ternary relationship does not mean that binary relationships among the entities may not exist. Using a similar example of CUSTOMERS, VENDORS, and PRODUCTS, suppose retail vendors and suppliers of products have a special relationship that does not involve customers — such as wholesaling with an entirely different price structure. This binary relationship can be shown separately from, and in addition to, a ternary relationship. See Figure 7.4 for a basic version of this two-way (binary) relationship and three-way (ternary) relationship ER diagram in the same database.

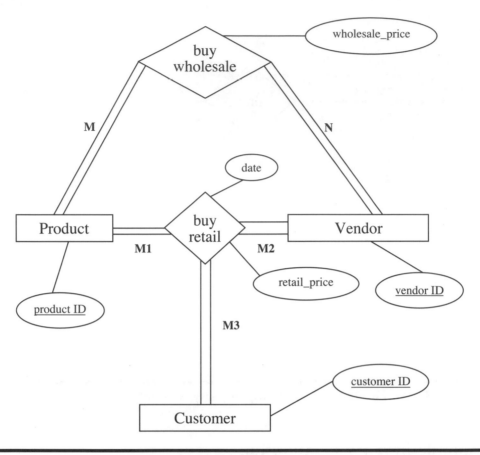

Figure 7.4   An ER Diagram (with Only Primary Keys) Showing a Three-Way and a Two-Way Relationship

The semantics of Figure 7.4 tell us that we have a binary relationship, buy wholesale, between PRODUCT and VENDOR, with all PRODUCTs and VENDORs participating. Both the VENDOR and the CUSTOMER *buy* the PRODUCT, but in the VENDOR/PRODUCT relationship, the action is wholesale buying and hence the relationship is labeled *buy wholesale*. We changed the ternary relationship to read *buy retail* to distinguish the two relationships.

Methodology and Grammar for the *n*-ary Relationship

We need to revisit step 6 in the ER design methodology to cover the possibility of the *n*-ary relationship. The old version was:

Step 6: State the exact nature of the relationships in structured English from all sides. For example, if a relationship is A:B::1:M, then there is a relationship from A to B, 1 to Many, and from B back to A, Many to 1.

We add the following sentence to step 6:

For ternary and higher-order (n-ary) relationships, state the relationship in structured English, being careful to mention all entities for the n-ary relationship. State the structural constraints as they exist.

The grammar for the *n*-ary relationship must involve all of the entities linked to it and, therefore, a suitable informal sentence would go something like this:

> ENTITY1 Relationship (from/to/by) ENTITY2 (and) (from/to/by) ENTITY3. It is understood that attribute will necessitate naming all n entities to identify it.

Here, if we choose some combination for Entity1, ..., Entity*n*, this process resolves into:

> Entity1 : CUSTOMER
> Relationship: *buy*
> Relationship attribute: retail price
> Entity2: PRODUCT
> Entity3: SUPPLIER

'CUSTOMERS *buy* PRODUCTS from SUPPLIERS. It is understood that retail price will necessitate referencing all three entities to identify it.

With a binary relationship, we have to state two relationships. One would think that with ternary relationships, we would be bound to state three. Because the relationship attribute has already been stated, let us look at the other possibilities:

> Entity1: CUSTOMER
> Entity2: SUPPLIER
> Entity3: PRODUCT
> CUSTOMERS *buy* from SUPPLIERS, PRODUCTS.

For the same value of Entity1, the sense of the statement is really repeated and adds no information to the process. Suppose that:

> Entity1: PRODUCT
> Entity2: CUSTOMER
> Entity3: SUPPLIER
> PRODUCTS are bought by CUSTOMERS from SUPPLIERS.

In the informal version of the statement from the diagram, little information is gained by repetition. It is suggested that other combinations be tried. But, in the informal statement, it seems likely that one statement, inferred from the semantics of the situation, would suffice to informally declare the nature of the relationship.

The More Exact Grammar

A more exact grammar for the *n*-ary relationship would be an extension of that developed for the binary relationship. Unlike the informal case above, in a more formal grammatical presentation, it would be necessary to make three statements (ternary), one starting with each entity. In the binary relationship, M:N, full participation case, we used the following description of the relationship:

Pattern 3 — M:N, from the M side, full participation

> *Short:* x must be related to many y

which actually means:

> *Long:* x, which are recorded in the database, must be related to many (one or more) y. No x is related to a non y (or) Non x are not related to a y. (The negative will depend on the sense of the statement).

We could generalize the structural constraint patterns to this:

Pattern 4 — k:M, from the k side, full participation (k = 1 or M)

> *Short:* same as above.

> *Long:* same as above.

For the *n*-ary relationship, we extend the notation of the generalized statement using the boolean operator, "and," like this:

Pattern 5 (n-ary) — x:y:z::a:b:c, from the a side, full/partial participation

> *Short:* x must/may be related to many y and many z.

The "must" comes from full participation; "may" comes from a partial one. The "a" cardinality will not matter. The "b" and "c" force us to say "one" or "many" in the statement. So, for example, for x as full:

> *Long:* x, which are recorded in the database, must be related to:

> b = m [many (one or more)] y

> b = 1 one and only one y

> and (or other appropriate linking word [from, by, to, …])

c = m [many (one or more)] z

c = 1 one and only one z.

No x is related to more than one z.

No x is related to more than one y.

Example

For CUSTOMERS:PRODUCTS:VENDORS::M1:M2:M3, full participation all around:

Short: CUSTOMERS must buy many PRODUCTS from many VENDORS.

Long: CUSTOMERS that are recorded in the database must buy many (one or more) PRODUCTS from many (one or more) VENDORS.

Other grammatical expressions are derived similarly:

Products, that are recorded in the database, must be bought by many (one or more) customers from many (one or more) vendors.

Vendors, that are recorded in the database, must sell many (one or more) products to many (one or more) customers.

A negative could be: No customer (in this database) buys products from nonvendors.

As with the binary cases, the negative statements would be optional, if they make sense.

Grammar in a Partial Participation, Ternary Relationship with a 1-Relationship

Now consider Figure 7.5. In this figure, we are trying to represent a database about a graduation ceremony that has some students and some faculty attending. Roughly, we are trying to say that some STUDENTS *attend* a given GRADUATION with some FACULTY; some FACULTY *attend* a GRADUATION with some STUDENTS; and all GRADUATIONs are *attend*ed by some STUDENTS and some FACULTY. The intersection attribute is derived attendance.

Here, we have some partial participations and a 1-relationship. Using the grammar presented above, we have the following outcome:

STUDENT:GRADUATION:FACULTY::M:1:M

Short: Students may attend one graduation with many faculty.

Long: Students, that are recorded in the database, may attend (b = 1) one and only one graduation.

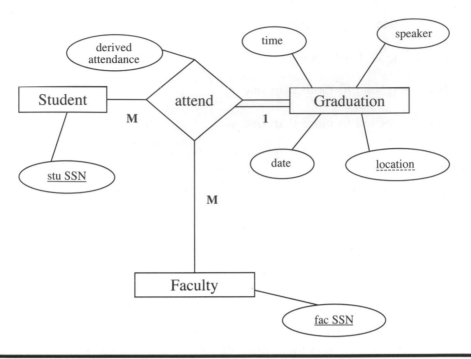

Figure 7.5   An ER Diagram (with Only Primary Keys) Showing a Three-Way Relationship with Partial Participations, and a 1-Relationship

with

(c = m) many (one or more)] faculty.

No student attends more than one graduation [with many faculty].

We put the [with many faculty] in square brackets because it is not really needed to make sense of the diagram.
   Similarly:

Faculty that are recorded in the database may attend one graduation with many students. Some faculty do not attend graduation [with many students].

Graduations must be attended by some students and some faculty. No graduation takes place without some students and some faculty.

Ternary Relationships from Relationship–Relationship Situations

Another scenario in which ternary relationships become necessary is where we have a scenario developing that results in a relationship of a relationship. Chen-like ER diagrams do not allow relationships of relationships; so, to represent this situation correctly, we need to develop a ternary relationship.

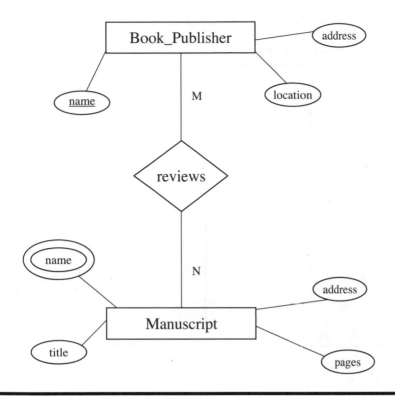

Figure 7.6A A Binary Relationship of BOOK_PUBLISHER and MANUSCRIPT

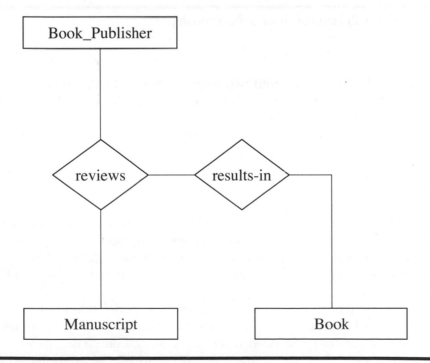

Figure 7.6B A Relationship of a Relationship

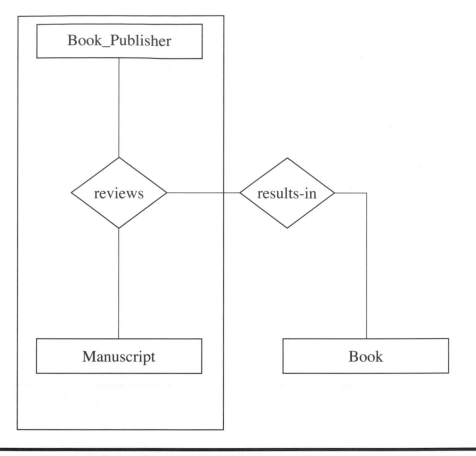

Figure 7.6C   A Relationship of a Relationship

For example, let us start with two entities: BOOK_PUBLISHER and MANU-SCRIPT. We can initially relate the two entities as shown in Figure 7.6A. A BOOK_PUBLISHER reviews a MANUSCRIPT.

At a later stage, if some MANUSCRIPTs result-in a BOOK after being reviewed, this calls for a relationship of a relationship, as shown in Figure 7.6B. This relationship of a relationship becomes necessary here because the BOOK_PUBLISHER, *review*, and MANUSCRIPT *taken together* will *result-in* a BOOK, as shown in Figure 7.6C.

In Figure 7.6C, this BOOK_PUBLISHER, the *reviews* relationship, and MANUSCRIPT *taken together* is like creating a higher-level aggregate class composed of BOOK_PUBLISHER, *review*, and MANUSCRIPT. This aggregate class (of the two entities and a relationship) then needs to be related to BOOK, as shown in Figure 7.6C.

To represent this situation correctly in the ER model schema presented in this book, and because we cannot show a relationship of a relationship to represent this situation, we need to create a weak entity (i.e., REVIEW) and relate it to BOOK_PUBLISHER, MANUSCRIPT, and BOOK as shown in Figure 7.6D. The intersection attribute, *BMR,* has to have a BOOK_PUBLISHER,

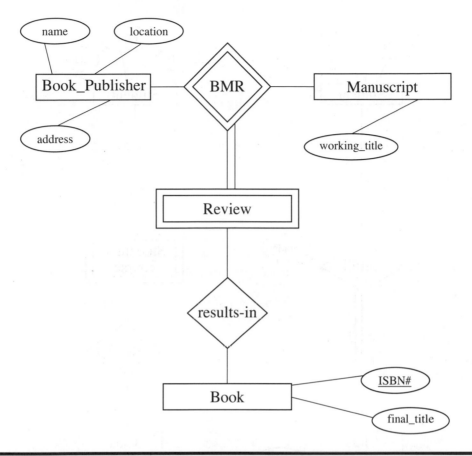

Figure 7.6D   A Relationship of a Relationship Resolved into a Ternary Relationship

MANUSCRIPT, and REVIEW. This review may *results-in* a BOOK (as shown in Figure 7.6D).

n-ary Relationships that May Be Resolved into Binary Relationships

Just because three entities are related does not necessarily imply a ternary relationship. In this section, we show how some ternary relationships can be resolved into binary relationships, and then we give another example of how a ternary relationship *cannot* be resolved into binary relationships (a real ternary relationship).

Just as the binary M:N relationship can be decomposed into two 1:M relationships, so can many *n*-ary relationships be decomposed. First, note the decomposition of the M:N into two 1:M's in Figure 7.7. The idea is to make the relationship an entity, and hence form two simpler binary relationships.

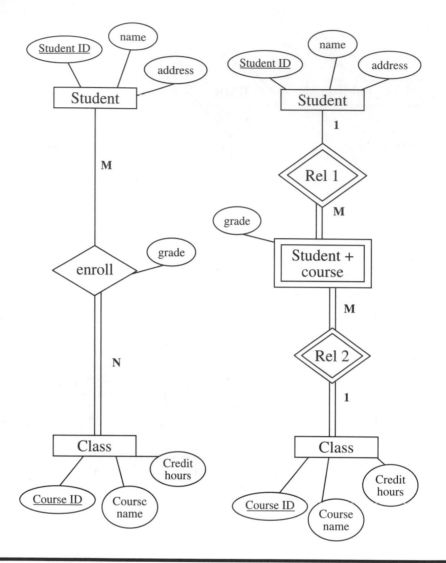

Figure 7.7   An ER Diagram of an M:N Relationship That Has Been Replaced with Two 1:M Relationships

Next, look again at Figure 7.5. If we decompose Figure 7.5 into three binary relationships, we obtain Figure 7.8. In Figure 7.8, note that the new entity ATTENDANCE is weak and depends on the three entities — FACULTY, STUDENT, and GRADUATION — for its existence. The sense of ATTENDANCE would be a roll of attendees for a GRADUATION ceremony event.

There are situations, however, in which a relationship inherently associates more than two entities. Take Figure 7.2 as an example. Here, if we had another attribute like an *order* that a customer places to a supplier for a product, this attribute would require all three entities (i.e., CUSTOMER, PRODUCT, and SUPPLIER) at the same time. An *order* would specify that a supplier would supply some quantity of a product to a customer. This

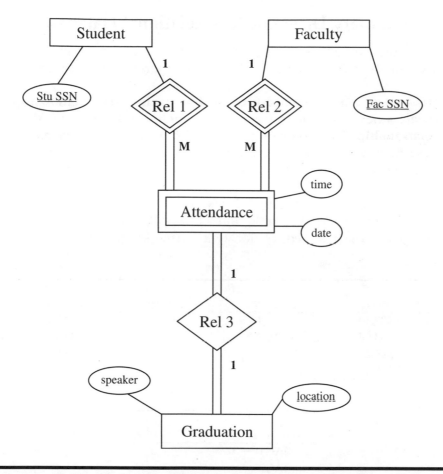

Figure 7.8 An ER Diagram (with Only Primary Keys) Showing a Three-Way Relationship "Decomposed" into Three Binary Relationships

relationship cannot adequately be captured by binary relationships. With binary relationships we can only say that a customer placed an order for a product, or a supplier received an order for a product. The fact that a customer places an order for a product does not imply that the customer C is getting the product P from a supplier S unless all three entities are related.

Checkpoint 7.2

1. Can all ternary relationships be expressed in the form of binary relationships? Explain.
2. Come up with some attributes and entities of a relationship that you think could be a ternary relationship. Can this relationship be expressed in the form of a binary relationship?

Mapping Ternary Diagrams to a Relational Database

In this section we develop mapping rules to map *n*-ary relationships to a relational database because this will also cover ternary relationships.

> **M6 — For *n*-ary relationships — For each *n*-ary relationship, create a new relation. In the relation, include all attributes of the relationship. Then include all keys of connected entities as foreign keys and make the concatenation of the foreign keys the primary key of the new relation. Qualify all foreign keys.**

For example, referring to Figure 7.2, you have a ternary relationship called *buy* relating PRODUCT, SUPPLIER, and CUSTOMER. There is an intersection attribute, price. The mapped relation (with some sample data) would be:

		BUY	
price	*productID*	*supplierID*	*customerID*
$87.10	TAG1	F1	PENS
$83.98	TAG2	G25	MOB
$95.25	TAG3	G20	DEL
$99.10	TAG4	F4	GULF

PRODUCT	
productID	...
TAG1	
TAG2	
TAG3	
...	

SUPPLIER	
supplierID	...
F1	
G25	
G20	
...	

CUSTOMER	
customerID	...
PENS	
MOB	
DEL	
...	

Checkpoint 7.3

1. Could Figure 7.3 be described in the form of binary relationships? Discuss.
2. What mapping rules would you follow to map Figure 7.3?
3. Map Figure 7.3 to a relational database and show some sample data.

Our ER design methodology has now finally evolved to the following:

ER Design Methodology

Step 1: Select one primary entity from the database requirements description and show attributes to be recorded for that entity. Label keys if appropriate and show some sample data.

Step 2: Use structured English for entities, attributes, and keys to describe the database that has been elicited.

Step 3: Examine attributes in the existing entities (possibly with user assistance) to find out if information about one of the entities is to be recorded.

(We change "primary" to "existing" because we redo step 3 as we add new entities.)

Step 3a: If information about an attribute is needed, make the attribute an entity, and then

Step 3b: Define the relationship back to the original entity.

Step 4: If another entity is appropriate, draw the second entity with its attributes. Repeat steps 2 and 3 to see if this entity should be further split into more entities.

Step 5: Connect entities with relationships (one or more) if relationships exist.

Step 6: State the exact nature of the relationships in structured English from all sides. For example, if a relationship is A:B::1:M, then there is a relationship from A(1) to B(M) and from B(M) back to A(1).

For ternary and higher order (n-ary) relationships, state the relationship in structured English, being careful to mention all entities for the n-ary relationship. State the structural constraints as they exist.

Step 6a: Examine the list of attributes and determine whether any of them need to be identified by two (or more) entities. If so, place the attribute on an appropriate relationship that joins the two entities.

Step 6b: Examine the diagram for loops that might indicate redundant relationships. If a relationship is truly redundant, excise the redundant relationship.

Step 7: Show some sample data.

Step 8: Present the "as-designed" database to the user, complete with the English for entities, attributes, keys, and relationships. Refine the diagram as necessary.

Chapter Summary

Binary relationships are, by far, the most commonly occurring kind of relationships, and some ER diagram notations do not have expressions for ternary or other, higher-order relationships; that is, everything is expressed in terms of a binary relationship. In this chapter we showed how the need for ternary relationships arises from unique situations; for example when there is an intersection attribute that needs all three entities together, or when relationships of relationships develop. Ternary relationships can also be developed through reverse-engineering, and this is discussed in Chapter 9 where reverse-engineering is discussed. Also in this chapter, we discussed in detail the structural constraints of ternary relationships and their grammar, and showed how some ternary or *n*-ary relationships can be resolved into binary relationships, but how some cannot be resolved into binary relationships. The final section of this chapter discussed mapping rules of *n*-ary relationships.

Chapter 7 Exercises

Exercise 7.1

In Chapter 5 we described a database that had two entities: COURSE and INSTRUCTOR. "Book" was left as an attribute of COURSE. Extend the database to include book as an entity. Attributes of book might include: book title, author, price, edition, and publisher. Explore the relationships that might exist here; use "in" or "by," "write," "teach," etc. Draw an ER diagram with at least two relationships, one of them ternary. What would be some attributes of the relationships?

Exercise 7.2

Construct an ER diagram for a broker, a security, and a buyer. Include in the diagram the price of the security, the commission paid, the broker name and address, the buyer name and address, and the security exchange, symbol, and price. Include in the diagram the number of shares of the security held by a buyer (you may choose to include this by broker, or not).

Exercise 7.3

Using three entities — INSTRUCTOR, CLASS, and ROOM — draw an ER diagram that depicts the following: Each CLASS in a ROOM has one INSTRUC-TOR, but each INSTRUCTOR in a room may have many CLASSes, and each INSTRUCTOR of a CLASS may be in many ROOMs.

References

Elmasri, R. and Navathe, S.B., *Fundamentals of Database Systems*, 3rd ed., Addison Wesley, Reading, MA, 2000.

Teorey, T.J., *Database Modeling and Design*, Morgan Kaufman, San Francisco, 1999.

Teorey, T.J., Yang, D., and Fry, J.P., "A Logical Design Methodology for Relational Databases Using the Extended Entity-Relationship Model," *ACM Computing Surveys*, 18(2), 197–222, June 1986.

Chapter 8

Generalizations and Specializations

Chapter Topics

In the first several chapters of this book, we presented the ER diagram as a conceptual database tool. The approach taken in developing an ER diagram was to assume that we were to model reality for a user. Although we worked on the basics of the ER diagram, there are situations where the basic model fails to completely describe the reality of the data to be stored. With the increase in the types of database applications, the basic concepts of ER modeling (as originally developed by Chen) were not sufficient to represent the requirements of more complex applications, such as generalizations and specializations (class hierarchies). An ER model that supports these additional semantic concepts is called the Enhanced Entity Relationship (EER) model (Elmasri and Navathe, 2000). This chapter discusses generalizations and specializations in the EER model and develops a methodology and grammar for this extension.

What Is a Generalization or Specialization?

The EER model includes all the concepts of the original ER model and additional concepts of generalization/specialization. Generalizations and specializations are associated with the concepts of superclasses and subclasses and attribute inheritance.

The concept of classes includes the use of simple attributes we have seen. In programming, the concept of a class also includes actions that a class may perform. As with data typing, databases tend to focus more on attributes than procedural action. The idea of classes also refers to the ability to describe subclasses and superclasses with inheritance features. For example, a STUDENT entity contains information about students. However, suppose we wanted to store information about all people at an institution — not only students, but also staff and faculty. We might think of a superclass called PERSON that contained a subclass for STUDENT, another subclass for STAFF, and yet another subclass for FACULTY. Clearly, information about each of these subclasses of PERSON contains information pertinent to that subclass. Yet, the superclass PERSON entity would contain information common to all of these subclasses. PERSON may contain a name, address, and phone number; and when the subclass STAFF was defined, it would inherit those attributes of the superclass and define more attributes pertinent to STAFF. The superclass in a database is called a generalization, and the subclasses (student, staff, and faculty) are called specializations.

A Problem with Variants

To visualize a problem with ER diagrams at this stage, suppose we are gathering facts about the database and we have reached a point where one of the attributes for an entity has values that vary according to "the situation." For example, suppose we are modeling student athletes who may play more than one sport. We would, of course, record information about the student — a name, a unique identifier such as a student number, perhaps some other information. But then we would like to record some information about the sports that the students may play. As an example, let us suppose that we have a student athlete "table" with this type of data:

| | | ATHLETE | | |
student	student #	other	sport	info
Baker	123456789	...	tennis	220, state rank 14
Adams	123456788	...	football	tackle, neck brace
Jones	123455676	...	golf	handicap 3

Some information in the ATHLETE entity contains attributes that have different values for different sports. These different values are called "variants." This variant problem in data processing has been solved in various ways over the years. A solution to the problem of variants in records and varying attributes in entities in the ER diagram is to excise the variant and reference it back to the primary key of the "parent" information piece.

In ER diagrams, we recognize that we are actually storing information about two different, but related, things: (1) a generalization called, "students," who have a name, id, etc.; and (2) specializations — sports (tennis, football, golf, etc.), each with their own different attributes. And because we are storing information about two things, why not create an entity called SPORTS and then relate the STUDENT to the SPORTS entity? One SPORTS entity would not work because the SPORTS entity would be general and we would want to store information about different, specific sports. Furthermore, what we want is to store information about sports as they pertain to each individual student.

Why then would we not create a series of weak entities — one for each sport, that depends on STUDENT? The answer is that we could do this, but there is a better way to look at this problem that, as it turns out, will result in the same database as using a weak entity relationship, but provides an alternative way to present the information with more expressive diagrams, to include the concept of inheritance.

Example of a Generalization or Specialization

Specializations and generalizations are categorizations of entities where the specialization entity might result from generalizations containing variants. These variants are most easily handled by removing the variant from the generalization and treating it as a subclass entity and leaving the original, "fixed part" of the entity as a superclass or "parent" type. If we referred to the superclass as a parent class, then we would call the variant parts, the subclasses, the "child classes."

Pursuing the parent-child superclass/subclass idea a bit further, we can imagine the child class inheriting the characteristics of the parent class. Inheritance in this context means that the child class will have defined in it whatever attributes are defined in the parent class. In our sports example, we would consider the STUDENT as a parent class and SPORTS as a child class so that when we define information about a sport, it is done in the context of the parent–STUDENT.

If we were designing the database for STUDENT–ATHLETES, as above, and we recognized that we would want to record a name, a personal identifier (a SS#), address, etc., we could be starting with the generalization (or parent or superclass). Then we decide to record a player in a sport and some information about the sport itself. The player-sport is said to be a specialization of the student class. This design approach may be characterized as "top down."

If we had been designing the database and we started with sports, we might have had a TENNIS entity, a FOOTBALL entity, etc. for each athlete, only to recognize that these entities may be generalized into a PERSON entity (a superclass) with individual sports as subclass-entities — this design approach might be characterized as "bottom-up." A generalization relationship specifies that several types of entities with certain common attributes can be generalized into a higher-level entity class, a generic or superclass entity.

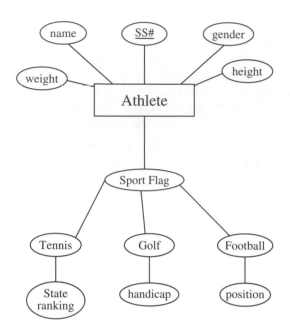

Figure 8.1   The Student–Athlete with an Attempt to Add a Variant Attribute

Either way (*bottom up* or *top down*), we end up with one entity being a superclass (a parent) and the other being a subclass (a child) of the parent. Whether one needs to specialize or generalize depends on where one recognizes the problem.

To illustrate how we might handle this generalization-specialization, parent-child class situation, suppose we have defined our entity, ATHLETE, like this:

Entity: ATHLETE
Attributes: name, SS#, address, gender, weight, height.

The ER diagram for this entity is simple and straightforward. Then, in the course of database design we decide to add information about sports that athletes play. We might attempt to draw a diagram like Figure 8.1 with the variant "Sports Flag."

What is wrong with Figure 8.1? The problem is that we have attributes that have attributes that have attributes. "Sports Flag" is not a composite name; it does not have component parts. Instead of creating attributes with attributes, we will create entities for each specific sport, and then relate these entities back to the ATHLETE.

Now refer to Figure 8.2. Here we have created weak entities for each sport. Actually, if the sports were real entities, we would have to make them weak because they depend on ATHLETE for their existence — they have no primary key. But we are not going to show the sports entities as weak, but rather we will use another notation which implies inheritance.

The process of specialization is intended as a process whereby the subclass inherits all the properties of the superclass. The player–sports entities would

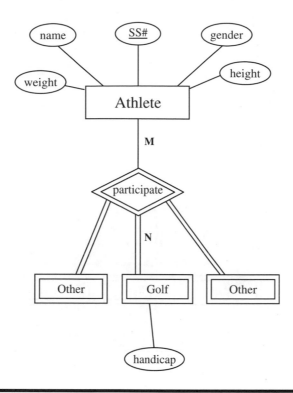

Figure 8.2   The Student–Athlete Shown as a Strong–Weak Relationship Variant Attribute

not make sense if standing alone and hence a tie back to the defining superclass is necessary. In EER terminology, the ATHLETE entity is called a superclass and the SPORTS entities are called subclasses. The attributes like handicap can be termed "specific attributes" as they are specific to the particular subclass. In other words, each member of a subclass is also a member of the superclass. The subclass member is the same as the entity in the superclass but has a distinct role.

The sports entities, "specializations," are depicted in the EER scheme as illustrated in Figure 8.3. In Figure 8.3, we have made the three sports entities unto themselves — information pieces that we want to store information about.

First, in the ATHLETE entity, we include an attribute called sport. Sport is called a "defining predicate" as it defines our specializations. Referring to Figure 8.3A, the defining predicate can be written on the line that joins the ATHLETE entity to the circle with an "o" in it. The circle with an "o" in it describes an "*overlapping* constraint." If there is an "o" in the circle, then this means that the subclass entities that are joined to it may overlap; that is, a superclass entity may be a member of more than one subclass of a specialization. So, the overlap ("o") in Figure 8.3A means that an athlete can participate in more than one sport, which means, an athlete can play tennis and golf; or golf and football; or golf, tennis, and football.

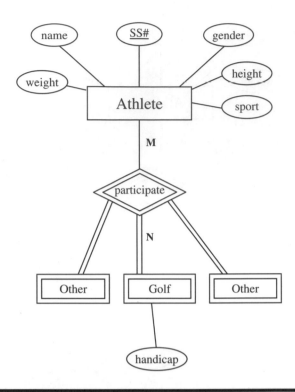

Figure 8.3   The Student–Athlete Shown as a Strong–Weak Relationship Variant Attribute

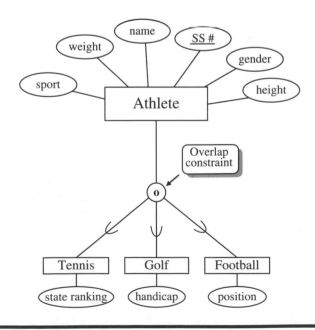

Figure 8.3A   The Student–Athlete Shown in a Superclass/Subclass Relationship

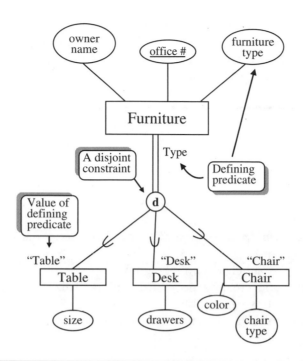

Figure 8.4   An Office Database with Specialization Entities, Full Participation and Disjoint

If there were a "d" in the circle (in place of the "o") in Figure 8.3A, then the entities would not overlap; they would be *disjoint*. A "d" would indicate that athletes could participate in only one sport; that is, the athletes could play only golf, or only tennis, or only football (but not any of the two together). As another example, if we had not used sports as a defining predicate, but rather used "state born in," the entities for "states born in" would have to be disjoint because a person could only be represented in one of the specialization (subclass, child) entities. An example of a disjoint constraint is shown in Figure 8.4.

According to Figure 8.4, all the furniture in the database is either a chair, a desk, or a table. All? Note the full participation designation from the FURNITURE entities to the circle and contrast this to the partial participation in the STUDENT-ATHLETE example. The disjoint constraint specifies that if the subclasses of a specialization are disjoint, then an entity can be a member of only one of the subclasses of the specialization.

In addition to the inclusion of the defining predicate, values of the defining predicate can be placed near the entity. This is not absolutely necessary and it may be redundant as in this case with the name of the specialization entity itself.

Figure 8.3A shows a subclass symbol (⊂) between the predicate-defined entities and the disjointness/overlapping constraint circle — "Tennis," "Golf," and "Football" belong to the defining predicate, "Sport." The entities, TENNIS, GOLF, and FOOTBALL are subclasses of ATHLETE. The subclass symbol on each line that connects a subclass to the circle indicates the direction of the superclass/subclass or parent-child, inheritance relationship. In Figure 8.3, the subclasses, TENNIS, or GOLF, or FOOTBALL (the specializations), would inherit from the parent, ATHLETE.

Checkpoint 8.1

1. What is a specialization? Come up with another example of a specialization.
2. What is a generalization? Come up with another example of a specialization.
3. What is a disjoint constraint? What symbol shows the disjoint constraint in EER diagrams?
4. What is an overlap constraint? What symbol shows the overlap constraint in EER diagrams?
5. What does the subclass symbol signify?
6. Why would you create a generalization/specialization relationship rather than creating a "weak entity?
7. How does "inheritance" play into the superclass/subclass relationship? Discuss.

Methodology and Grammar for Generalization/ Specialization Relationships

We need to revisit step 6 in the ER Design Methodology to cover the possibility of generalization/specialization relationships. The previous version of step 6 was:

Step 6: State the exact nature of the relationships in structured English from all sides. For example, if a relationship is A:B::1:M, then there is a relationship from A to B, 1 to Many, and from B back to A, Many to 1.

For ternary and higher-order (*n*-ary) relationships, state the relationship in structured English, being careful to mention all entities for the *n*-ary relation. State the structural constraints as they exist.
We add the following sentence to step 6:

For specialization/generalization relationships, state the relationship in structured English, being careful to mention all entities (subclasses or specializations). State the structural constraints as they exist.

The grammar that we propose for specializations/generalizations relationships is similar to that we used in weak relationships. We add to the grammar to include the participation, overlapping/disjointness constraints:

The grammatical description for weak entities was:

For each *weak entity,* we do not assume that any attribute will be unique enough to identify individual entities. Because the *weak entity* does not have a candidate key, each *weak entity* will be identified by key(s) belonging to the *strong entity*.

In the case of our athlete, a first attempt to describe the subclass identified by a superclass becomes:

For each ATHLETE in a SPORT, we do not assume that any sport attribute will be unique enough to identify individual SPORT entities. Because the SPORT does not have a candidate key, each SPORT will be identified by inheriting key(s) belonging to ATHLETE.

So, a more complete EER diagram grammatical pattern would say:

For each *specialization*, we do not assume that any attribute will be unique enough to identify individual entities. Because the *specialization* does not have a candidate key, each *specialization* will be identified by key(s) inherited from the *generalization*. Further, *specializations overlap [or are disjoint]*. [Explain the overlap/disjoint feature]. The individual *specialization* is identified by a defining predicate, *attribute name*, which will be contained in *generalization*.

For Figure 8.3A, the pattern becomes:

For each sport, we do not assume that any attribute will be unique enough to identify individual entities. Because the sport does not have a candidate key, each sport will be identified by key(s) inherited from ATHLETE. Further, the sports overlap. Athletes may play more than one sport. The individual sport is identified by a defining predicate attribute (sport) that will be contained in ATHLETE. The sports we will record are golf, tennis, and football.

Mapping Rules for Generalizations and Specializations

In this section we present mapping rules to map generalizations and specializations to a relational database:

M7 — For each generalization/specialization entity situation, create one table for the generalization entity (if you have not done so already per the earlier steps) and create one table for each specialization entity. Add the attributes for each entity in their each respective tables. Add the key of the generalization entity into the specialization entity. The primary key of the specialization will be the same primary key as the generalization.

For example, refer to Figure 8.3A. The generalization/specialization relationship between the ATHLETE and TENNIS, GOLF, and FOOTBALL would be mapped as follows:

| | | ATHLETE | | | |
weight	name	gender	height	SS#	sport
140	Kumar	M	5.95	239–92–0983	golf
200	Kelvin	M	6.02	398–08–0928	football
135	Sarah	F	5.6	322–00–1234	tennis
165	Arjun	M	6.01	873–97–9877	golf
145	Deesha	F	5.5	876–09–9873	tennis

| | TENNIS | |
ss#	state ranking	national ranking
322–00–1234	23	140
876–09–9873	47	260

| GOLF | |
ss#	handicap
239–92–0983	3
873–97–9877	1

| FOOTBALL | |
ss#	position
398–08–0928	tackle
239–92–0983	quarter back
398–08–0928	full back

The key of the generalization entity (ss#) is added to the specialization entities TENNIS, GOLF, FOOTBALL. ss# also becomes the primary key of the specialization entities.

So, our ER design methodology (with one component of the EER model — the generalization/specialization component) has finally evolved to the following:

ER Design Methodology

Step 1: Select one, primary entity from the database requirements-description and show attributes to be recorded for that entity. Label keys if appropriate and show some sample data.

Step 2: Use structured English for entities, attributes, and keys to describe the database that has been elicited.

Step 3: Examine attributes in the existing entities (possibly with user assistance) to find out if information about one of the entities is to be recorded.

(We change "primary" to "existing" because we redo step 3 as we add new entities.)

Step 3a: If information about an attribute is needed, make the attribute an entity, and then

Step 3b: Define the relationship back to the original entity.

Step 4: If another entity is appropriate, draw the second entity with its attributes. Repeat steps 2 and 3 to see if this entity should be further split into more entities.

Step 5: Connect entities with relationships (one or more) if relationships exist.

Step 6: State the exact nature of the relationships in structured English from all sides. For example, if a relationship is A:B::1:M, then there is a relationship from A(1) to B(M) and from B(M) back to A(1).

For ternary and higher-order (n-ary) relationships, state the relationship in structured English, being careful to mention all entities for the n-ary relationship. State the structural constraints as they exist.

For specialization/generalization relationships, state the relationship in structured English, being careful to mention all entities (subclasses or specializations). State the structural constraints as they exist.

Step 6a: Examine the list of attributes and determine whether any of them need to be identified by two (or more) entities. If so, place the attribute on an appropriate relationship that joins the two entities.

Step 6b: Examine the diagram for loops that might indicate redundant relationships. If a relationship is truly redundant, excise the redundant relationship.

Step 7: Show some sample data.

Step 8: Present the "as designed" database to the user, complete with the English for entities, attributes, keys, and relationships. Refine the diagram as necessary.

Checkpoint 8.2

1. How are the mapping rules for generalizations/specializations different from the mapping rules for weak entities?
2. Map Figure 8.4 to a relational database and show some sample data.

Chapter Summary

In this chapter we described the concepts of specialization/generalization. The concepts of overlap and disjoint were also presented. This chapter approached EER diagrams as discussed by Elmasri and Navathe (2000) and Connolly et al. (1998). Some authors, for example Sanders (1995), use a close variation of this model, and call the specialization/generalization relationship an "IsA" relationship. Although we do not discuss "unions" and "categories," "hierarchies and lattices," these are further, uncommon extensions of a generalization/specialization relationship as presented by Elmasri and Navathe (2000).

This chapter also concluded the development of the EER design methodology. In the next chapter we will discuss mapping ER and EER diagrams to the relational model as well as reverse-engineering.

Chapter 8 Exercises

Exercise 8.1

Draw an ER diagram for a library for an entity called "library holdings." Include as attributes the call number, name of book, author(s), and location in library. Add a defining predicate of "holding type," and draw in the disjoint, partial specializations of journals and reference books, with journals having the attribute "renewal date" and reference books having the attribute "checkout constraints." Map this to a relational database and show some sample data.

Exercise 8.2

Draw an ER diagram for computers at a school. Each computer is identified by an id number, make, model, date acquired, and location. Each computer is categorized as a student computer or a staff computer. For a student computer, an attribute is "hours available." For a staff computer, an attribute is "responsible party" ("owner" if you will). Map this to a relational database and show some sample data.

References

Connolly, T., Begg, C., and Strachan, A., *Database Systems, A Practical Approach to Design, Implementation, and Management,* Addison-Wesley, Harlow, England, 1998.

Elmasri, R. and Navathe, S.B., *Fundamentals of Database Systems,* 3rd ed., Addison-Wesley, Reading, MA, 2000.

Sanders, L., *Data Modeling,* Boyd & Fraser Publishing, Danvers, MA, 1995.

Teorey, T.J., *Database Modeling and Design,* Morgan Kaufman, San Francisco, CA, 1999.

Case Study:
West Florida Mall (continued)

Thus far in our case study, we have developed the major entities and relationships, and mapped these to a relational database (with some sample data). Then, upon reviewing step 7, which says:

Step 7: Present the "as-designed" database to the user, complete with the English for entities, attributes, keys, and relationships. Refine the diagram as necessary.

Suppose we obtained some additional input from the user:

> A PERSON may be an owner, employee, or manager. For each PERSON, we will record the name, social security number, address, and phone number.

Upon reviewing these additional specifications, we came up with one new entity, PERSON.

Now, repeating step 2 for PERSON:

The Entity

> This database records data about a PERSON. For each PERSON in the database, we record a person's name (pname), person's social security number (pssn), person's phone (pphone), and person's address (padd).

The Attributes for PERSON

> For each PERSON there will always be one and only one pname (person's name) recorded for each PERSON. The value for pname will not be subdivided.

> For each PERSON, there will always be one and only one pssn (person's social security number) recorded for each PERSON. The value for pssn will not be subdivided.

> For each PERSON there will always be one and only one pphone (person's phone) recorded for each PERSON. The value for pphone will not be subdivided.

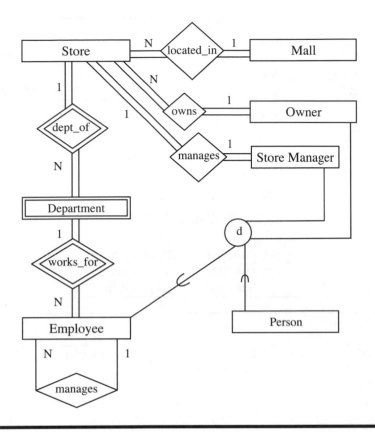

Figure 8.5   An ER Diagram of West Florida Mall Developed Thus Far

For each PERSON there will always be one and only one padd (person's address) recorded for each PERSON. The value for padd will not be subdivided.

The Keys

For each PERSON, we will assume that the pssn will be unique.

These entities have been added to the diagram in Figure 8.5.
Using step 6 to determine the structural constraints of relationships, we get:
As shown in Figure 8.5, there is a disjoint relationship between PERSON and STORE MANAGER, OWNER, and EMPLOYEE. This means that a person may be an owner, store manager, or an employee (a disjoint generalization/specialization relationship).

To Map This Relationship (with some sample data):

EMPLOYEE			
essn	*dnum*	*snum*	*dm_ssn*
987–754–9865	501	1	276–263–9182
276–263–9182	502	1	null
982–928–2726	503	1	987–754–9865

STORE MANAGER	
sm_ssn	*salary*
234–987–0988	45,900
456–098–0987	43,989
928–982–9882	44,000

OWNER	
so_ssn	*so_off_phone*
879–987–0987	(850)474–2093
826–098–0877	(850)474–9873
928–088–7654	(850)474–9382

PERSON			
pssn	*pname*	*padd*	*pphone*
879–987–0987	Earp	1195 Gulf Breeze Pkwy, Pensacola, FL	(850)837–0982
826–098–0877	Sardar	109 Navy Blvd, Pensacola, FL	(850)987–0373
928–088–7654	Bagui	89 Highland Heights, Tampa, FL	(813)938–0383
987–754–9865	Miller	55 Neverland, Pace, FL	(850)897–5633
276–263–9182	Foyer	109 Pace Blvd, Mobile, AL	(251)464–3117
982–928–2726	Khanna	503 Wildwood Land, Columbus, OH	(330)664–7654
234–987–0988	Bush	100 Indian Road, North Canton, OH	(330)865–9843
456–098–0987	Rodgers	398 Southern Street, Detroit, MI	(776)875–9754
928–982–9882	Bundy	387 Bancroft Street, Toledo, OH	(419)536–4374

Because PERSON has the fields of social security number (pssn), name (pname), address (padd), and phone number (pphone), and because a person may be an owner, store manager, or an employee — a disjoint, generalization/specialization relationship, notice that we removed some of the attributes from the original entities. For example, in the EMPLOYEE entity, we no longer need to keep the ename field because this can be obtained from PERSON, as long as we have the ss# of the employee.

So, in summary, our relational database would finally develop to (without the data):

MALL–Store

name	store_name

MALL

name	address

STORE

sloc	sname	snum	mall_name	so_ssn	sm_ssn

OWNER

so_ssn	so_off_phone

DEPARTMENT

dname	dnum	snum

EMPLOYEE

essn	dnum	snum	dm_ssn

PERSON

pssn	pname	padd	sport	pphone

This ends our case study.

Chapter 9

Relational Mapping and Reverse-Engineering ER Diagrams

Chapter Topics

Throughout this book we developed the rules for mapping an ER diagram to a relational database. In this chapter we present a summary of the mapping rules, and then discuss reverse-engineering.

We often find that databases exist without an accompanying ER diagram. The ER diagram is documentation; and just as computer programs require documentation, so do databases. Therefore, we have included a section on reverse-engineering ER diagrams; that is, working from a relational database back to an ER diagram. For reverse-engineering, we present a series of steps to develop a diagram from the data.

Steps Used to Map an ER Diagram to a Relational Database

Presented here is a summary of the steps needed to map an ER diagram to a relational database. In following these rules, the resulting relational tables should be close to 3NF. However, these rules do not preclude the exercise of checking the resulting database to be absolutely sure it is normalized. This is reassuring in a way, in that even if the mapping rules are misapplied, there is still one last chance to ensure a 3NF relational database.

Step 1: Map the strong entities in the ER diagram.

> **M1 — For strong entities — create a new table (relation) for each strong entity and make the indicated key of the strong entity the primary key of the table. If more than one candidate key is indicated on the ER diagram, choose one as the primary key for the table.**

Next we have to map the attributes in the strong entity. Mapping rules are different for atomic attributes, composite attributes, and multi-valued attributes. First, the mapping rule for mapping atomic attributes:

> **M1a — Mapping atomic attributes from an entity — For entities with atomic attributes: Map entities to a table (relation) by forming columns from the atomic attributes for that entity.[1]**

What about the composite and multi-valued attributes? In relational database, all columns have to be atomic. If we have a non-atomic attribute on our diagram, we have to make it atomic for mapping to the relational database. For composite attributes, we achieve atomicity by recording only the component parts of the attribute. Our next mapping rule concerns composite attributes:

> **M1b — For entities with composite attributes, form columns from the elementary (atomic) parts of the composite attributes.**

The mapping rule for multi-valued attributes is:

> **M1c — For multi-valued attributes, form a separate table for the multi-valued attribute. Include the primary key from the original table. The key of the new table will be the concatenation of the multi-valued attribute plus the primary key of the owner entity. Remove the multi-valued attribute from the original table.**

Step 2: Map the weak entities in the ER diagram.

> **M4 — For Weak Entities — Develop a new table for each weak entity. As is the case with the strong entity, include the attributes in the table using rules M1a, M1b, and M1c. To relate the weak entity to its owner, include the primary key of the owner entity in the weak table as a foreign key. The primary key of the weak table will be the partial key in the weak entity concatenated to the key of the owner entity.**

---

[1] These mapping rules are adapted from Elmasri and Navathe (2000).

If weak entities own other weak entities, then the weak entity that is connected to the strong entity must be mapped first. The key of the weak owner entity has to be defined before the "weaker" entity (the one furthest from the strong entity) can be mapped.

Step 3: Map the binary M:N relationships.

M3a — For binary M:N relationships — For each M:N relationship, create a new relation with the primary keys of each of the two entities (owner entities) that are being related in the M:N relationship. The key of this new relation will be the concatenated keys of each of the two owner entities. Include any attributes that the M:N relationship may have in this new relation.

Step 4: Map the binary 1:1 relationships — the Primary key/ Foreign key method.

There are two ways to map any relationship. A new table can be created as in rule M3a; or, with non-M:N relationships, the relationship can be mapped by a primary key/foreign key (PK/FK). To use the PK/FK technique:

M3b — For binary A:B::1:1 relationships — include the primary key of EntityA into EntityB as the foreign key.

The question is: which is EntityA and which is EntityB? This question is answered in the next three mapping rules, M3b_1, M3b_2, and M3b_3, which take participation into account:

M3b_1 — For binary 1:1 relationships, *if one of the sides has full participation in the relationship*, and the other has partial participation, then store the primary key of the side with the partial participation constraint on the side with the full participation constraint. Include any attributes on the relationship in the table that gets the foreign key. Note that this rule will result in no null values for the foreign key.

M3b_2 — For binary 1:1 relationships, *if both sides have partial participation constraints*, there are three alternative ways to implement a relational database:

M3b_2a — First alternative: you can select either one of the tables to store the key of the other (and live with some null values).

M3b_2b — Second alternative: depending on the semantics of the situation, you can create a new table to house the relationship that would contain the key of the two related entities (as is done in M3a).

M3b_2c — Third alternative: create a new table with just the keys from the two tables in addition to the two tables. In this case we would map the relations as we did in the binary M:N case; and if there were any null values, these would be left out of the linking table.

M3b_3 — For binary 1:1 relationships, *if both sides have full participation constraints*, you can use the semantics of the relationship to select which table should contain the key of the other. It would be inappropriate to include foreign keys in both tables as you would be introducing redundancy in the database. Include any attributes on the relationship, on the table that is getting the foreign key. This situation may be better handled using the new table rule M3a.

Step 5: Map the binary 1:N relationships.

M3c — Although most binary 1:N relationships are mapped with the PK/FK method, the separate table per rule M3a can be used. To use the PK/FK method for binary 1:N relationships, we have to check what kind of participation constraints the N side of the relation has:

M3c_1 — For binary 1:N relationships, if the N-side has full participation, include the key of the entity from the 1 side in the table on the N side as a foreign key in the N side table. If the N side is weak with no primary key, a key from the 1 side will be required in the N side table concatenated to the weak partial key. The key of this table will be the weak partial key plus the foreign key. Include any attributes that were on the relationship, in the table that is getting the foreign key (the N side).

M3c_2 — For binary 1:N relationships, if the N side has partial participation, the 1:N relationship is best handled just like a binary M:N relationship with a separate table for the relationship to avoid nulls. The key of the new table consists of a concatenation of the keys of the related entities. Include any attributes that were on the relationship, on this new "intersection table."

Partial participation is a problem because it leads to null values. If we put the key from the 1 side into the N-side relation, and if the participation is partial (not every tuple on the N side has a relationship to the 1 side), then there will be nulls in the database when it is populated. Therefore, it is better to create a separate table for the 1:N relationship and hence avoid nulls.

Finally, on the subject of 1:N relationships, we should look back at Figure 6.2 where an M:N relationship was converted into two 1:N relationships. Note that the result of converting the M:N into two 1:N relationships will result in the same set of tables from the 1:N mappings.

Step 6: Map recursive relationships.

M5 — For recursive entities, two types of mapping rules have been developed:

M5a — For 1:N recursive relationships, reinclude the primary key of the table with the recursive relationship in the same table, giving the key some other name.

M5b — For M:N recursive relationships, create a separate table for the relationship (as in mapping rule M3a).

Step 7: Map n-ary (higher than binary) relationships.

M6 — For *n*-ary relationships — For each *n*-ary relationship, create a new table. In the table, include all attributes of the relationship. Then include all keys of connected entities as foreign keys and make the concatenation of the foreign keys the primary key of the new table.

Step 8: Map generalizations/specializations.

This is most often a situation where you have an entity set with variants — attributes that apply to some occurrences and not others. The concept of inheritance applies in that it is assumed that each derived subclass inherits the properties of the "superclass" or "parent."

M7 — For each generalization/specialization entity situation, create one table for the generalization entity (if you have not done so already per steps 1 through 7) and create one table for each specialization entity. Put the attributes for each entity in the corresponding table. Add the primary key of the generalization entity into the specialization entity. The primary kcy of the specialization will be the same primary key as the generalization.

Checkpoint 9.1

1. What is the first mapping rule?
2. How would you map weak entities of weak entities?
3. While mapping a binary 1:N relationship where the N side has full participation, why do we include the key of the 1 side of the relation in the N side of the relation? What would be wrong if we included the key of the N side of the relation in the 1 side of the relation?
4. Why would it be reasonable to map a 1:N binary relationship that has partial participation on the N side like a M:N relationship?

If the above rules were followed, the resulting relational database should be at or close to 3NF. The next phase of mapping is "checking your work" by reviewing the tables to ensure that you are at least in 3NF (refer to Chapter 1). In brief, checking for 3NF consists of the following steps:

1. **1NF** — Check that there are no non-atomic attributes in any table. Non-atomic attributes were dealt with in steps M1b for composite attributes and M1c for multi-valued attributes.

2. **2NF** — Check that all attributes in all tables depend on the primary key. Ask yourself, "Will I always get the same value for attribute Y when I have value X where X is the primary key?"

3. **3NF** — Check for situations where an attribute is in a table but that attribute is better defined by some attribute that is not the primary key. Recall that if the primary key in a table is X and X → YZW, then if Z → W is better than X → W, you likely have a transaction dependency and you need to normalize.

Reverse-Engineering

Having developed a methodology to develop ER diagrams and map them to a relational database, we now turn our attention to the reverse problem: the issue of taking a relational database and coming up with an ER diagram. Often in real-world situations, we find ourselves with a database and we have no diagram to show how it was developed. There are several reasons why a reverse-engineered diagram (RED) paradigm is useful.

First, the RED provides us with a grammatical and diagrammatic description of the database. People often use databases but do not understand them. By reverse-engineering from the data and tables to the diagram, we can more easily express the meaning of the database in words. By having the ER diagram of the relational database and the grammatical expression of the diagram, we can embellish the database and maintain meaning. We can also aid in the development of queries on the database.

While the expression "reverse-engineering" might imply that we reverse the steps to create a diagram, we have found it easier to repeat the steps from the top (more or less) to discover what diagram would have been used to create the relational database. There is one caveat here, in that the steps presented assume that the database is in 3NF. If it is not in 3NF, reverse-engineering may aid in discovering why redundancy exists in the database and hence suggest some changes. We suggest the following:

Rule R1: Develop strong entities

For tables with a one-attribute key, draw a strong entity R for that table and include all the attributes of that table on the entity R on the ER diagram.

For example, if you have a table, R($\underline{a}$,b,c,d,e), $\underline{a}$ is the key. Create a strong entity called R and show a, b, c, d, and e as attributes with a as the key. See Figure 9.1.

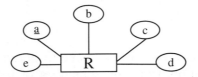

Figure 9.1   Reverse-Engineering Strong Entities

R

a	b	c	d	e

Rule R2: Look for 1:1 and 1:N (1:x) relationships

As second, third, … strong entities are discovered, note foreign keys in the tables found previously; excise the foreign keys from the previous table and create a relationship between the entities. This situation would have indicated a 1:x relation.

For example, in addition to the above, if you have another table, S, S(d,f,g). d is the key of S and is in R, so d is a foreign key in R. Remove d from R (see Figure 9.2), giving:

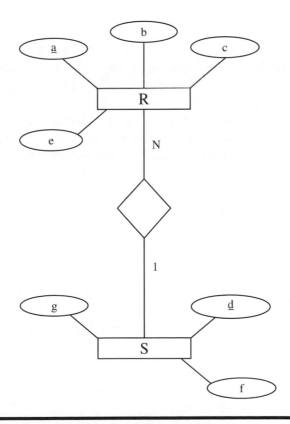

Figure 9.2   Reverse-Engineering 1:N Relationships

R($\underline{a}$,b,c,e)

S($\underline{d}$,f,g)

In all cases of relationships, we may have to determine the cardinality and the participation constraints from the semantics of the database. Sometimes, the way that the tables are formed provides a clue. Also, sample data may help in elucidation. For example, if the tables are as the above case, then it is likely that the relationship was N:1, with the N side being R because R contained d, a foreign key. The data can be examined to determine if any nulls are present, which would indicate a partial participation (note carefully that we are saying "indicate" because only the true [albeit unknown] semantics would "prove" the full participation).

Rule R2a: Check for attributes of the 1:x relationships

If a foreign key is excised from a relation R because it is the key of S, you have to check to see whether any of the remaining attributes in R should stay with the relation R, or should be placed on a relationship RS, or should be placed with S. Because step 2 is reverse-mapping a 1:x relation, it may be that an attribute from the 1:x relation itself was placed with the foreign key when the original ER diagram was mapped, or it may be that an attribute was on the relationship itself.

You have to judge where a remaining attribute is more likely to belong. If it is likely that the attribute was defined by the key of an entity, put the attribute with the entity containing the key. If the attribute requires both keys for its identity, the attribute should be placed on the relation RS for sure.

For example, in the above, if we removed d from R because d was the key of S. Suppose that e was better defined by d (the key of S) than $\underline{a}$ (the key of R). If this is true, then e should be placed with S and removed from R. This would result in:

R($\underline{a}$,b,c)

S($\underline{d}$,f,g,e)

Example R2a2: In the above, we removed d from R because d was the key of S. Suppose that after we create S, we determine that e only makes sense if we define it in terms of both a and d, the keys of R and S. This would imply that e was an intersection attribute on the relationship between R and S, and hence would be depicted as such (see Figure 9.3).

R ($\underline{a}$,b,c)

S ($\underline{d}$,f,g,e)

RS ($\underline{a}$,$\underline{d}$,e)

This concludes the reverse-mapping of obviously strong relations. We will now look for weak relations and multi-valued attributes.

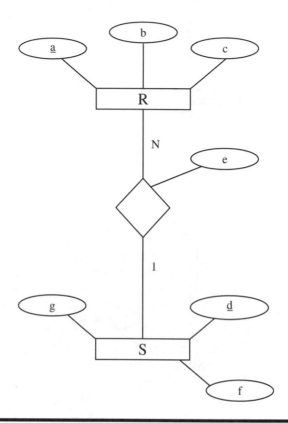

Figure 9.3   An ER Diagram Showing the Relationship between R and S

Rule R3: Look for weak entities or multi-valued attributes.

Examine the relations for any concatenated keys to see whether they contain any of the keys of the strong entities. If they do, this could indicate a weak entity (rule R3a), a multi-valued attribute (rule R3b), or a table resulting from M:N relationship. Which of these it is will depend on non-key attributes.

Rule R3a: Weak entities

If there is a table where there are attributes other than the key (which consists of a foreign key from a strong entity *and* another attribute - the partial key), then you probably have a weak entity. For example, if you have a table:

```
SKILL (emp#, skill type, date_certified)
```

Here, emp# is a foreign key, skill_type is not, and hence would likely be a partial key of a weak entity. Why a weak entity? Because there is another attribute, date certified, that means we are storing information about SKILL.

Place the weak entity on the ER diagram along with a relationship to its owner entity. The relationship is likely to be 1:N::strong(owner):weak(dependent)::partial:full. Examine the attributes in the weak entity to determine

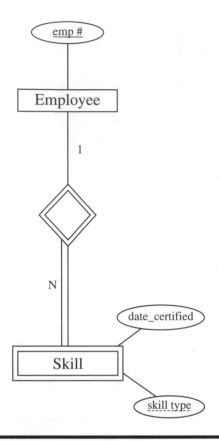

Figure 9.4   Reverse-Engineering Weak Entities

whether they would have come from the weak entity or the relationship between the weak entity and its owner. Here, SKILL is the weak entity, skill_type is the partial key, and date certified is an attribute of the entity SKILL (see Figure 9.4).

Rule R3b: Multi-valued attributes

If there are no attributes other than the key in a relation and the part of the key is a foreign key from a strong entity, it is likely a multi-valued attribute that would have been connected to the strong entity referenced by the foreign key. Place the multi-valued attribute on the entity to which it belongs as a multi-valued attribute.

For example, if we have the relation:

```
INSTRUCTOR (SS#, degree)
```

Here, we have a concatenated key and no other attributes. Because SS# is likely the key of another entity (e.g., PERSON), then degree must be a multi-valued attribute. Why not a weak entity? Because, if there were a weak entity, there would probably be more attributes — for example, we would be

Figure 9.5   Reverse-Engineering Multi-Valued Attributes

recording information about the degrees but we are not in this case doing so. Figure 9.5 diagramatically shows the reverse of engineering of the multi-valued attribute example discussed above.

Rule R4: M:N and n-ary relationships

Examine the relations for multiple occurrences of primary keys from the entities derived thus far. Remember that a weak entity has a concatenated key, so an M:N relationship from Strong:Weak will have more than two attributes participating in the key.

Rule R4a: The binary case

If there are two foreign keys by themselves in a table (and nothing else), this is likely a table that occurred because of a relationship. If the two foreign keys occur with other attributes, it is even more likely that an M:N relationship existed along with attributes of the relationship. Place an M:N relationship between the two entities with foreign keys and include other attributes as relationship attributes.

For example, if you discover a relation called PURCHASE which looks like this (see Figure 9.6):

PURCHASE (<u>vendor#, part#</u>, price)

Suppose vendor# is the key of an entity called VENDOR and part# is the key of an entity called PART. These two foreign keys are a clear message that this is a table formed from an M:N (or possibly a 1:N or even a 1:1) relationship. The M:N is most likely and the relationship can be deduced from the data. If, for example, there are multiple occurrences of parts for vendors and vice versa, this is an M:N. If, for every part, there is a list of vendors but every vendor supplies only one part, then this would be VENDOR:PART::N:1.

Rule R4b: n-ary case

If there are more than two foreign keys in a relation participating as the key of the relation, this is likely a relation that occurred because of an *n*-ary relationship. There may well be other attributes in the relation with the three or more foreign keys. Place an *n*-ary relationship (*n* = number of foreign keys) between the *n* entities with foreign keys and include other attributes as relationship attributes.

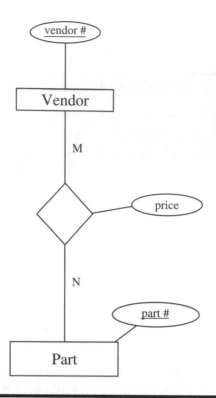

Figure 9.6   Reverse-Engineering M:N Relationships

For example, consider the following relation:

> PURCHASE (<u>vendor#, part#, cust#,</u> price)

Three foreign keys imply a ternary relationship. The attribute price is likely an intersection attribute on the relationship. In this case, we would be saying that all three keys would be necessary to identify a price, as shown in Figure 9.7.

Checkpoint 9.2

1. What hints would you look for to determine if a relationship is ternary?
2. What hints would you look for when you are trying to determine whether relations have weak entities and multi-valued attributes included in them?

Chapter Summary

In this chapter we presented a summary of the mapping rules (rules used to map ER diagrams to relational databases) that we developed throughout the

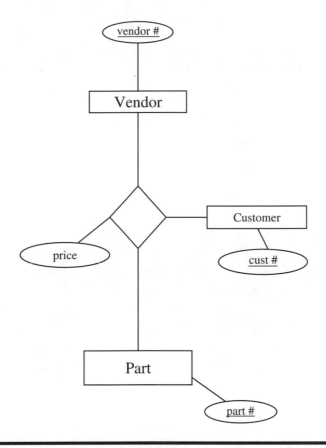

Figure 9.7   Reverse-Engineering *n*-ary Cases

book, and then discussed and developed a set of rules for reverse-engineering
to ER diagrams from a relational database.

Chapter 9 Exercises

Exercise 9.1

Come up with an ER diagram for the following relational database:

    R (a, b, c, d, w)
    S (d, e, f)
    T (c, g, h)
    U (c, d, j)
    V (d, k)
    W (a, m, o, p)
    X (a, d, c, r)
    Y (a, o, s, t)

References

Elmasri, R. and Navathe, S.B., *Fundamentals of Database Systems*, 3rd ed., Benjamin Cummings, Redwood City, CA, 2000.

Chapter 10

A Brief Overview of the Barker/Oracle-Like Model

Chapter Topics

There are many variations (models) of ER diagrams. One such model was introduced by Richard Barker (1990). The Barker model was adopted and modified slightly by the Oracle Corporation. In this chapter we introduce the conventions used in the Barker/Oracle-like model as it applies to our ER design methodology. We are going to depict major concepts of both Barker and Oracle's ER diagrams. Our combined Barker/Oracle-like model is not meant as a primer on either party's "pure model," but the transition to Barker or Oracle's ER diagrams will be minor.

Why are we interested in the Barker/Oracle-like model and why present it here? First, the Barker/Oracle-like model is common; it is used often in Oracle literature. The pedantic problem with the Barker/Oracle-like model is that one needs to fully understand relational database theory to understand why the Barker/Oracle-like model is done the way it is. We present the Barker/Oracle-like model here because the way it unfolds is a bit different from the Chen-like model. The Chen-like model focuses on modeling data, whereas the Barker/Oracle-like model adapts the data to the relational database concurrently with the design. Therefore, the ER design methodology for the Barker/Oracle-like model will develop differently from the Chen-like model. Further, the Barker/Oracle-like model does not have some of the conventions used in the Chen-like model. For example, the Barker/Oracle-like model does not directly use the concept of composite attributes, multi-valued attributes, or weak entities, but rather handles these concepts immediately in light of the relational model. Because the Barker/Oracle model is so close to the relational model to begin with, the mapping rules are trivial — the mapping takes place in the diagram itself.

A First "Entity-Only" ER Diagram — An Entity with Attributes

We start with developing a first, "entity-only" ER diagram in the Barker/Oracle-like model. To recap our example used earlier in the book, we have chosen a "primary" entity from a student-information database — the STUDENT. A "student" is something that we want to store information about (the definition of an entity). For the moment we will not concern ourselves with any other entities.

What are the some initial attributes we used in the STUDENT? A student has a name, address, school, phone number, and major. We have picked five attributes for the entity STUDENT, and have also chosen a generic label for each: name, address, school, phone, and major.

We begin our venture into the Barker/Oracle-like model with Figure 10.1. A Barker/Oracle-like model uses soft boxes for entities (with the entity name in capital letters), and there is a line separating the entity name from the attributes (and the attribute names are in lowercase letters). A Barker/Oracle-like model does not place the attributes in ovals (as the Chen-like model does), but rather lists the attributes below the entity name, as shown in Figure 10.1.

Figure 10.1 shows an ER diagram with one entity, STUDENT, and the following attributes: name, address, school, phone, and major. In the Oracle-

Figure 10.1   Barker/Oracle-Like Notation: An ER Diagram with One Entity and Five Attributes

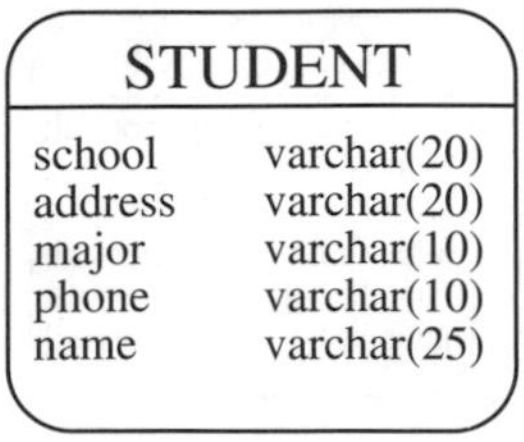

Figure 10.1A   Barker/Oracle-Like Notation: An ER Diagram with One Entity and Five Attributes (Data Types Added)

like version of the Barker/Oracle-like ER diagram, the data type is also listed — see Figure 10.1A.

Attributes in the Barker/Oracle-Like Model

All attributes in a Barker/Oracle-like model are considered simple or atomic, as in relational databases. The Barker/Oracle-like model does not have the concept of composite attributes. So, our Barker/Oracle-like adaptation will show parts of the composite attributes using a dot (.) notation, as shown in Figure 10.2.

Optional versus Mandatory Attributes

When designing a database, it is necessary to know whether or not an entity can contain an unknown value for an attribute. For example, in the STUDENT entity (shown in Figure 10.1), suppose that the address was optional. That is, if data was recorded for a student on a paper data entry form, we could demand that the person fill out his name and student number but allow him to have the address blank (i.e., unknown). We would say that the name and the student number are "mandatory," and address is "optional." A missing value is called a "null." Hence, the mandatory attribute is said to be "not null." Not null means that on *no* occasion would an instance of the entity exist without knowing the value of this mandatory attribute. In the Barker/Oracle-like ER model, we will show the optional attribute without the "not null"

Figure 10.2   Barker/Oracle-Like Notation: An ER Diagram with a Composite Attribute — name

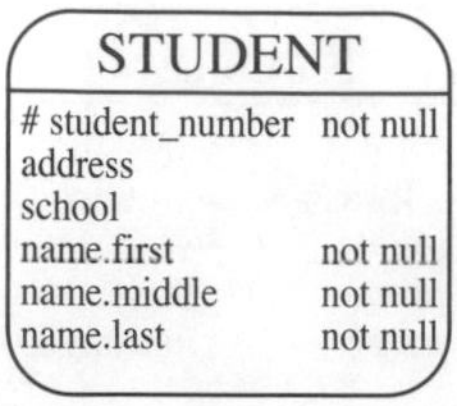

Figure 10.3   Barker/Oracle-Like Notation: An ER Diagram with a Primary Key or Unique Identifier Attribute and Optional and Mandatory Attributes

depiction and the mandatory attribute by adding the phrase "not null" to the description (as shown in Figure 10.3). A mandatory attribute could be a key but it is not necessarily a key. Mandatory and optional attributes are usually not indicated explicitly in the Chen-like model.

In our Barker model, the primary key has a " # " in front of the name of the attribute (as shown in Figure 10.3). A primary key has to be a mandatory attribute in a relational database, but again, all mandatory attributes here are not necessarily unique identifiers.

Checkpoint 10.1

1. What do mandatory attributes (in the Barker/Oracle-like model) translate into in the Chen-like model? Discuss with examples.
2. What do optional attributes (in the Barker/Oracle-like model) translate into in the Chen-like model? Discuss with examples.
3. How are the primary keys being shown diagrammatically in the Barker/Oracle-like model?

Relationships in the Barker/Oracle-Like Model

In the Barker/Oracle-like model, a relationship is represented by a line that joins two entities together. There is no diamond denoting the relationship (as we saw in the Chen-like model). The relationship phrase for each end of a relationship is placed near the appropriate end (entity) in lower case, as shown in Figure 10.4. In this model, from the STUDENT entity to the SCHOOL entity, we would say (informally) that:

> Students attended schools

And, from the other direction, from the SCHOOL entity to the STUDENT entity, we would say that:

> Schools are attended by students.

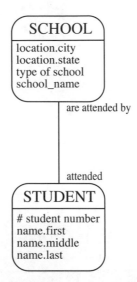

Figure 10.4   Barker/Oracle-Like Notation: The STUDENT Entity with a Relationship to the SCHOOL Entity

Structural Constraints in the Barker/Oracle-Like Model

In the Barker/Oracle-like notation, the cardinality of 1 is shown by a single line leading up to the entity. In Figure 10.5, a single line joins the two entities, so this is a 1:1 relationship between STUDENT and AUTOMOBILE. This means that one student can be related to one and only one automobile, and one automobile can be related to one and only one student.

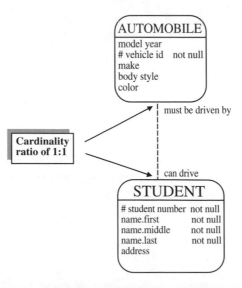

Figure 10.5   1:1 Relationship in the Barker/Oracle-Like Notation

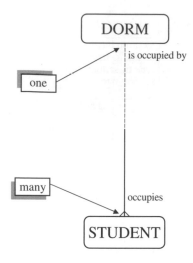

Figure 10.6   1:M Relationship in the Barker/Oracle-Like Notation

The dashed line leading up to an entity signifies optional (partial) participation of an entity in a relationship. In figure 10.5, both the STUDENT entity and the AUTOMOBILE entity are participating optionally in the relationship.

An enhanced grammar from the STUDENT entity to the AUTOMOBILE entity would be:

A student may drive one and only one automobile

And for the AUTOMOBILE entity to the STUDENT entity would be:

An automobile must be driven by one and only one student.

A continuous (solid) line coming from an entity (as shown in Figure 10.6) signifies mandatory (full) participation of that entity in a relationship. So, according to Figure 10.6, students **must** occupy dorms, but a dorm **may** have students.

A cardinality of M (many) is shown by "crowsfoot" structure leading to the respective entity. Figure 10.6 is an example of a 1:M relationship between DORM and STUDENT. The exact grammar of Figure 10.6 would be:

A dorm may be occupied by zero or more students

or

A student must occupy one and only one dorm.

Checkpoint 10.2

1. How is the "optional" relationship shown diagrammatically in the Barker/Oracle-like model?
2. How is the "many" relationship shown diagrammatically in the Barker/Oracle-like model?
3. Show the following using the Barker/Oracle-like notation:
   a. A movie theater must show many movies and movies must be shown in a movie theater.
   b. A movie theater may show many movies and movies may be shown in a movie theater.

Dealing with the Concept of the Weak Entity in the Barker/Oracle-Like Model

The Barker/Oracle models do not have a concept of the "weak entity," and the weak entity notation is not used in Oracle literature either. We will extend the concept of the unique identifier in a relationship to include the weak entity. In the Barker/Oracle-like model, the unique identifier in a relationship can be diagrammatically shown by a bar cutting across the contributing relationship, as shown in Figure 10.7. In Figure 10.7, to uniquely identify a dependent, one needs the employee's social security number. This means that the DEPENDENT entity cannot independently stand on its own, and hence is a weak entity. However, here the weak entity would be mapped as per the mapping rules discussed in Chapter 5.

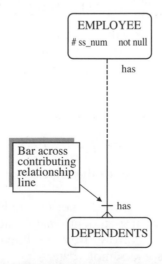

Figure 10.7   Unique Identifier Shown by Placing Bar across Contributing Relationship Line(s)

Dealing with the Concept of Multi-Valued Attributes in the Barker/Oracle-Like Model

Again, although the Barker/Oracle models do not have the concept of the "multi-valued" attribute, multi-valued attributes can be shown as in Figure 10.8.

Figure 10.8 shows that a student may have attended many schools. In the Barker/Oracle-like model, the foreign key is shown in the appropriate entity, whereas in the Chen-like model, foreign keys are not "discovered" until the database is mapped. We will signal a foreign key with an asterisk (*) in front of the attribute (see Figure 10.8). An instance of this database shown in Figure 10.8 is:

STUDENT	
sname	*address*
Sumona Gupta	111 Mirabelle Circle, Pensacola, FL
Tom Bundy	198 Palace Drive, Mobile, AL
Tony Jones	329 Becker Place, Mongotomery, AL
Sita Pal	987 Twin Lane, North Canton, OH
Neetu Singh	109 Bombay Blvd, Calicut, CA

SCHOOL	
sname	*school*
Sumona Gupta	Ferry Pass Elementary
Sumona Gupta	PCA
Sumona Gupta	Pensacola High
Tom Bundy	Mobile Middle School
Tom Bundy	St. Johns
Tony Jones	Montgomery Elementary
Tony Jones	Montgomery Middle
Tony Jones	Montgomery High
Sita Pal	Tagore Primary School
Sita Pal	Nehru Secondary School

As you can see, the multi-valued attribute is mapped to tables as it is depicted in the Barker/Oracle-like notation. In the Chen-like model, the multi-valued attribute is kept in the diagram and then mapped using the mapping rules (see mapping rule M1c).

Checkpoint 10.3

1. Does the Barker-like model or the Oracle-like model have the concept of the "weak entity"? Discuss.
2. Show the following using the Barker/Oracle-like notation: For a student, we are trying to store the student's name, address, phone, books (i.e., books that the student borrows from the library). Map this to a relational database and show some sample data.

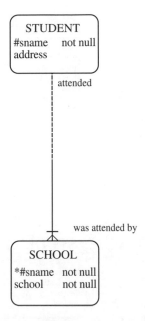

Figure 10.8   Unique Identifier Shown by Placing Bar across Contributing Relationship Line(s) [*Note:* "*" shows a foreign key.]

Treatment of Foreign Keys

In the original Barker model, foreign keys are not marked. In the Oracle model, however, foreign keys are included in the respective relations. For example, in Figure 10.9, which says:

> A student may drive many automobiles

and

> An automobile must be driven a student.

The primary key from the STUDENT relation (the 1 side), student number, is included in the AUTOMOBILE relation (the N side). In our Barker/Oracle-like model, we will precede the foreign key with an "*" (as shown in Figure 10.9).

Recursive Relationships in the Barker/Oracle-Like Model

Recursive relationships in the Barker/Oracle-like model are drawn as shown in Figure 10.10. Once again, the dotted line in the relationship shows an optional relationship, the solid line would show a mandatory relationship, and a "crowsfoot" would show a "many" relationship. The relationships are named as shown. Figure 10.10 shows that an employee may supervise other

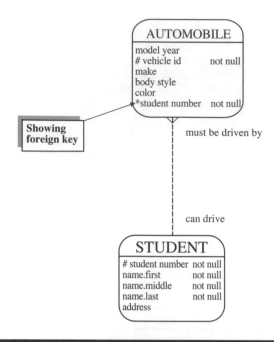

Figure 10.9   Barker/Oracle-Like Notation Showing Foreign Key

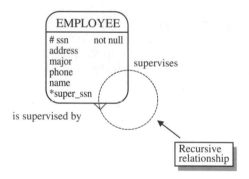

Figure 10.10   Barker/Oracle-Like Notation: Recursive Relationships

employees and an employee may be supervised by one and only one supervisor. Note the foreign key, super_ssn, in the EMPLOYEE relation itself.

Mapping M:N Relationships

Finally, we discuss one last important aspect that is treated differently in the Barker/Oracle-like model — an M:N relationship. In the Barker/Oracle-like model, all M:N relationships are resolved into two 1:M relationships with an intersection entity in the middle. In the Chen-like model, the M:N relationship can also be presented as two 1:M relationships.

Take Figure 10.11, for example (this is in the Chen-like format). In the Barker/Oracle-like model, this would be shown as in Figure 10.12.

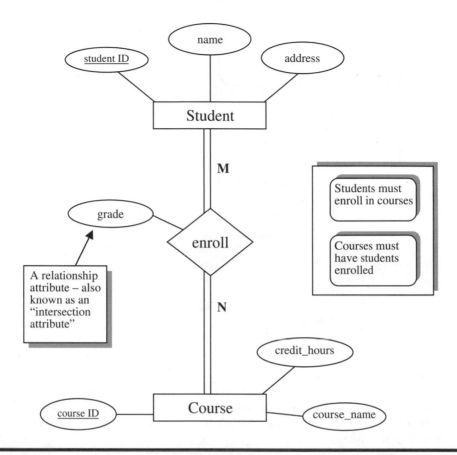

Figure 10.11   An ER Diagram of an M:N Relationship in the Chen-Like Model

---

Checkpoint 10.4

1. How are recursive relationships shown in the Barker/Oracle-like model?
2. Why is it difficult to show M:N relationships in the Barker/Oracle-like model?
3. How are the foreign keys treated in the Barker/Oracle-like model?

Chapter Summary

This chapter briefly discussed some of the main features of the Barker/Oracle-like model. The "one-entity" diagram, with attributes, was presented. The idea of optional versus mandatory attributes was discussed. Relationships and structural constraints were briefly discussed in the context of the Barker/Oracle-like model, and although the Barker/Oracle-like notation does not use the concept of the weak entity and multi-valued attributes, we showed how

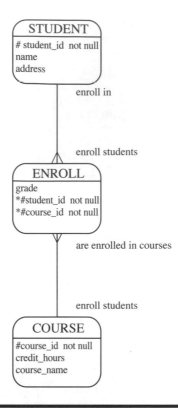

Figure 10.12   Barker/Oracle-Like Notation: M:N Relationship Broken into Two 1:M Relationships

these concepts can be shown diagrammatically in the Barker/Oracle-like notation. An example of the depiction of the recursive relationship in the Barker/Oracle model was illustrated. Finally, the chapter showed how to map an M:N relationship into two 1:M relationships. Mapping rules were also discussed in the context of Barker/Oracle-like notation.

Chapter 10 Exercises

Exercise 10.1

Redraw Figure 6.12A using the Barker/Oracle notation. Map this to a relational database and show some sample data.

Exercise 10.2

Redraw Figure 6.7 using the Barker/Oracle notation. Map this to a relational database and show some sample data.

References

Barker, R., *Case*Method, Entity Relationship Modelling*, Addison-Wesley, Reading, MA, 1990.

Hay, D.C., *Data Model Patterns*, Dorset House, New York, 1996.

Rodgers, Ulka, *ORACLE: A Database Developer's Guide*, Prentice Hall, Englewood Cliffs, NJ, 1991.

Glossary

A

Attribute: Property used to describe an entity or relationship.

B

Binary relationship: Relationship between two entities.

C

Candidate key: An attribute or set of attributes that uniquely identifies individual occurrences of an entity type.

Cardinality ratio: Describes the number of one entity that is related to another entity.

Composite attribute: An attribute composed of multiple components, each with an independent existence.

D

Database: A shared collection of logically associated or related data.

Degree of a relationship: The number of participating entities in a relationship.

Derived attribute: An attribute that gets a value that is calculated or derived from the database.

E

Entity: "Something" in the real world that is of importance to a user and that needs to be represented in a database so that information about the entity can be recorded. An entity may have physical existence (such as a student or building) or it may have conceptual existence (such as a course).

Entity set: A collection of all entities of a particular entity type.
Entity type: A set of entities of the same type.

F

First Normal Form (INF): Where the domain of all attributes in a table must include only atomic (simple, indivisible) values, and the value of any attribute in a tuple (or row) must be a single-valued from the domain of that attribute.
Foreign Key: An attribute that is a primary key of another relation (table). A foreign key is how relationships are implemented in relational databases.
Full participation: Where all of one entity set participates in a relationship.
Functional dependency: A relationship between two attributes in a relation. Attribute Y is functionally dependent on attribute X if attribute X identifies attribute Y. For every unique value of X, the same value of Y will always be found.

G

Generalization: The process of minimizing the differences between entities by identifying their common features and removing the common features into a superclass entity.

I

Identifying owner: The strong entity upon which a weak entity is dependent.
Identifying relationship: A weak relationship.

K

Key: An attribute or data item that uniquely identifies a record instance or tuple in a relation.

M

Mandatory relationship: Same as full participation; where all of one entity set participates in a relationship.
Many-to-many: Where many tuples (rows) of one relation can be related to many tuples (rows) in another relation.
Many-to-one: Where many tuples (rows) of one relation can be related to one tuple (row) in another relation.
Mapping: The process of choosing a logical model and then moving to a physical database file system from a conceptual model (the ER diagram).
Multi-valued attribute: An attribute that may have multiple values for a single entity.

One-to-many: A relationship where one tuple (or row) of one relation can be related to more than one tuple (row) in another relation.

One-to-one: A relationship where one tuple (or row) of one relation can be related to only one tuple (row) in another relation.

Optional participation: A constraint that specifies whether the existence of an entity depends on its being related to another entity via a relationship type.

P

Partial key: The unique key in a dependent entity.

Partial participation: Where part of one entity set participates in a relationship.

Participation constraints (also known as optionality): Determines whether all or some of an entity occurrence is related to another entity.

Primary key: A unique identifier for a row in a table in relational database; A selected candidate key of an entity.

R

Recursive relationship: Relationships among entities in the same class.

Regular entity: *See* Entity.

Relation: A table containing single-value entries and no duplicate rows. The meaning of the columns is the same in every row, and the order of the rows and columns is immaterial. Often, a relation is defined as a populated table.

Relationship: An association between entities.

S

Second Normal Form: A relation that is in first normal form and in which each non-key attribute is fully, functionally dependent on the primary key.

Simple attribute: Attribute composed of a single value.

Specialization: The process of maximizing the differences between members of a superclass entity by identifying their distinguishing characteristics.

Strong entity: An entity that is not dependent on another entity for its existence.

Structural constraints: Indicate how many of one type of record is related to another and whether the record must have such a relationship. The cardinality ratio and participation constraints, taken together, form the structural constraints.

Subclass: An entity type that has a distinct role and is also a member of a superclass.

Superclass: An entity type that includes distinct subclasses required to be represented in a data model.

T

Table: Same as relation; a tabular view of data that may be used to hold one or more columns of data; an implementation of an entity.

Third Normal Form: A relation that is in second normal form and in which no non-key attribute is functionally dependent on another non-key attribute (i.e., there are no transitive dependencies in the relation).

U

Unique identifier: Any combination of attributes and/or relationships that serves to uniquely identify an occurrence of an entity.

W

Waterfall model: A series of steps that software undergoes, from concept exploration through final retirement.

Weak entity: An entity that is dependent on some other entity for its existence.

Index

S